CHAPEL OF LOVE

American Made Music Series

Advisory Board

David Evans, General Editor
Barry Jean Ancelet
Edward A. Berlin
Joyce J. Bolden
Rob Bowman
Susan C. Cook
Curtis Ellison
William Ferris
John Edward Hasse
Kip Lornell
Bill Malone
Eddie S. Meadows
Manuel H. Peña
Wayne D. Shirley
Robert Walser

CHAPEL OF LOVE

The Story of New Orleans
Girl Group the
DIXIE CUPS

Rosa Hawkins and Steve Bergsman

University Press of Mississippi / Jackson

The University Press of Mississippi is the scholarly publishing agency of
the Mississippi Institutions of Higher Learning: Alcorn State University,
Delta State University, Jackson State University, Mississippi State University,
Mississippi University for Women, Mississippi Valley State University,
University of Mississippi, and University of Southern Mississippi.

www.upress.state.ms.us

The University Press of Mississippi is a member
of the Association of University Presses.

Copyright © 2021 by University Press of Mississippi
All rights reserved
Manufactured in the United States of America

First printing 2021

∞

All photographs are courtesy of Rosa Hawkins.

Library of Congress Cataloging-in-Publication Data

Names: Hawkins, Rosa, 1944– author. | Bergsman, Steve, author. | Vera, Billy, author of foreword.
Title: Chapel of love : the story of New Orleans girl group the Dixie Cups / Rosa Hawkins and Steve Bergsman.
Other titles: American made music series.
Description: Jackson : University Press of Mississippi, 2021. | Series: American made music series | Includes bibliographical references and index.
Identifiers: LCCN 2021006496 (print) | LCCN 2021006497 (ebook) | ISBN 9781496829566 (hardback) | ISBN 9781496834959 (epub) | ISBN 9781496834966 (epub) | ISBN 9781496834973 (pdf) | ISBN 9781496834980 (pdf)
Subjects: LCSH: Dixie Cups (Musical group) | African American women singers—Louisiana—New Orleans—Biography. | Women singers—Louisiana—New Orleans—Biography. | Singers—Louisiana—New Orleans—Biography.
Classification: LCC ML421.D5815 H38 2021 (print) | LCC ML421.D5815 (ebook) | DDC 782.42163092/2 [B]—dc23
LC record available at https://lccn.loc.gov/2021006496
LC ebook record available at https://lccn.loc.gov/2021006497

British Library Cataloging-in-Publication Data available

This book is dedicated to my mother, Mrs. Lucille Cordelia Merette Hawkins, who until her death was the single most influential person in my life. A proud, single mom who worked hard to give her daughters the things she didn't have growing up. A hardworking woman who instilled in me at an early age that reading was essential to my growth and development as a child and later as a young woman. She would always tell me how reading was not just about learning but a chance to experience diverse cultures, history, and places from around the world. The gifts I received from reading were the catalyst for my imagination and the drive for my career in entertainment. Thanks, Mom, for being you! Still reading today!

—**Rosa Hawkins**

CONTENTS

Foreword by Billy Vera ix

Preface xiii

CHAPTER ONE Sugah Wooga 3

CHAPTER TWO You Talk Too Much 15

CHAPTER THREE Marie Laveau 23

CHAPTER FOUR Thank You Mama, Thank You Papa 37

CHAPTER FIVE Chapel of Love 49

CHAPTER SIX People Say 61

CHAPTER SEVEN The House of the Rising Sun 77

CHAPTER EIGHT You Should Have Seen the Way He Looked at Me 93

CHAPTER NINE Iko Iko 107

CHAPTER TEN Walking to New Orleans 115

CHAPTER ELEVEN I'm Gonna Get You Yet 125

CHAPTER TWELVE When the Levee Breaks 133

CHAPTER THIRTEEN Little Bell 141

Notes 145

Discography 147

Selected Bibliography 149

Index 153

FOREWORD

The 1964 New York World's Fair was held at Flushing Meadows in the borough of Queens, the same location as the World's Fair of 1939.

One of the 140 pavilions was Louisiana's Bourbon Street Pavilion, inspired by the French Quarter of New Orleans. Among the ten theater restaurants, which all served that city's delicious Creole cuisine, was a nightclub called Jazzland, featuring miniature Mardi Gras parades, a voodoo shop, a doll museum, an old-time minstrel show produced by Mike Todd, and various homegrown jazz groups.

One of these latter was the rhythm and blues band of Joe Jones, whose hit record "You Talk Too Much" had been a big national hit in 1960. Musicians from all over the New York area, especially drummers, were flocking to Flushing Meadows to see this band, once word got out that someone was playing a rhythm previously unheard of north of New Orleans's city limits. The drummer was Charles "Honeyman" Otis, and local drummers knelt at his feet to catch the funky off-beats he played. Guitar players and bassists also came to see what the hell was going on. Jones's guitarist was one Alvin "Shine" Robinson, and the bass player is remembered today only as "Preacher."

This little band changed how New York musicians played music virtually overnight and soon came to the attention of songwriters/producers Jerry Leiber and Mike Stoller. The producers recorded Otis as "The Honeyman" on a song called "Brother Bill (The Last Clean Shirt)," and Robinson had a hit with Chris Kenner's "Something You Got," along with several wonderful sides like "How Can I Get Over You," "Down Home Girl," and a revival of Little Willie John's "Fever."

The big news, though, came from three little Crescent City girls that Jones brought to Leiber & Stoller's offices, called the Meltones. At this stage of their career, Jerry and Mike weren't much interested in teenage music. Their focus was more on the young adult sounds they had been making with the Drifters and Ben E. King, and they were talking about writing a Broadway show.

So, to keep their hands in the teenybopper marketplace, they hired a pair of staff songwriters, a married couple named Jeff Barry and Ellie Greenwich, to their publishing company, Trio Music. The couple had the knack for capturing the overwrought feelings and emotions of teenage girls and had a list of hits to show for themselves by the Crystals, the Ronettes, and other girl groups of the period.

Jeff and Ellie pulled a song out of the trunk that had been attempted by Phil Spector with his groups the Crystals and the Ronettes. But Spector's Wall of Sound didn't work with this plain tune, so they tried it a different way, soft and simple, with no lead singer, just basic harmony, sort of like the old Andrews Sisters, who'd been so popular during World War II.

It worked, and with a name change to the Dixie Cups, "Chapel of Love" lit up radio stations across America and rose to the top of the charts. More hits followed—"People Say," "You Should've Seen the Way He Looked At Me," and "Iko Iko"—before the British Invasion elbowed the Dixie Cups and most other American acts off the charts and into the dustbin of rock 'n' roll history.

During this period, my band and I served as the house band at a place called the Country House (later the Deercrest Inn) in the tiny hamlet of Banksville, New York, on the border of Greenwich, Connecticut. Each weekend we'd play two dance sets and back two shows featuring the hit record acts of the day. Most of these acts were in the $400 per night range, other than the bigger names, like the Coasters or the Drifters or the occasional Fats Domino or Jerry Lee Lewis. One of these $400 acts was the Dixie Cups. I remember them as shy, unassuming girls, not like the Ronettes or Patti LaBelle & the Bluebelles. They sang their songs and a few other hits of the day to fill their forty-minute set.

Their guitar player and conductor was the same Alvin Robinson whose records I'd bought and loved, so I got a big kick out of talking with him. I remember telling him I thought he was the one singer who came closest to Ray Charles of any who tried. He played a black and white Silvertone electric guitar, the same one I'd bought from Sears for $35 as a teenager. It sounded a lot better when he played it. He seemed surprised and flattered that anybody outside of his hometown knew who he was.

I loved "Chapel of Love" and still do for its lovely simplicity and tender sincerity, not to mention its memorable melody that is as good as anything Irving Berlin ever wrote. As much as any girl-group recording, this song stands the test of time. And don't forget that, in its time, people married young, in their early twenties or often right out of high school. Songs about marriage abounded and were aimed at young people who, a mere few years before, had been listening to first-generation rock 'n' roll, only hot rods and malt shops were now out, and marriage, jobs, and families were in.

This book tells the story of this song, these three girls, and the milieu in which they plied their craft and to which they gave their hearts, the proverbial good, the bad, and the very ugly . . . the snake pit that was the music business in the early 1960s.

—Billy Vera

PREFACE

After more than fifty years, one can still go to a concert and see the Dixie Cups perform. The group, as it was formed in New Orleans, consisted of Rosa Hawkins, her sister Barbara Hawkins, and cousin Joan Marie Johnson, who has since passed away. Rosa and Barbara now sing with Athelgra Neville, a friend since high school and sister of the famed singing family the Neville Brothers.

Although their career as recording artists was short, about a year in total, the Dixie Cups made a tremendous impact. Their first recording, "Chapel of Love," went to number one, and their reinterpretation of a New Orleans chant became "Iko Iko," a Mardi Gras staple and Crescent City favorite. They reached the pinnacle of the record charts during the heyday of what is known as the Girl Group Era, but they were different from the other girl groups in that they sang with a choral sound and not a format of call-and-response, or lead singer with background singers, which was popular at that time.

The Dixie Cups were also important for another reason. New Orleans has a long history of fostering the growth of rhythm and blues and rock 'n' roll. The city also has birthed an outsized array of musical talent, from Louis Armstrong to Fats Domino, from Sidney Bechet to Dr. John, and from Jelly Roll Morton to Aaron Neville. Notice that all these famous singers are male. The Dixie Cups were the first successful female singing group to come out of New Orleans in the last half of the twentieth century.

None of this was without a struggle. The three young ladies who became the original Dixie Cups suffered through terrible mismanagement and were abused financially, professionally, and sexually.

All that grief is the underlying reason this book was created. After keeping these terrible memories submerged and quiet, Rosa Hawkins wanted to finally see the true history of the Dixie Cups come to light.

That's how I became involved. I had interviewed Barbara and Rosa for another book I had been working on when Rosa said to me she wanted to write a memoir of her life and needed help. I had just come off working with Beverly Lee of the original Shirelles on her memoir and thought this would be an easy transfer. I had no idea of the strange series of circumstances that first fueled and then almost destroyed this glorious group of singers who became the Dixie Cups.

The book's creation process was long and encompassing. I interviewed Rosa for one-hour sessions, recording as she spoke, and then transcribed my tapes. This went on for almost a year. All Rosa's stories are the basis of the book, which is both a memoir and history of the Dixie Cups. My job was to neatly and accurately turn the oral into written words—and to put all that into the context of what was happening in the real world at that time and, most importantly, in the world of music at the time the events of Rosa's life unfolded.

Finally, a nod to Carolyn Thomas for internet research. Also to Barbara Hawkins for additional comments.

CHAPEL OF
LOVE

CHAPTER ONE

Sugah Wooga

Singing popular songs with other teenage girls, that wasn't me at all. That was my sister Barbara's thing. She did the Wa-Lo-Co (Walter Louis Cohn High School) talent show for two years. When it was my turn, I also did the Wa-Lo-Co, but I didn't sing. I was part of a troupe that square-danced. No one associated me with my sister Barbara; no one said to me, "Oh, your sister was such a good singer, what about you?"

Barbara and I lived in the same house and were very close, but some things we did together, and some things we didn't. When Barbara was competing at talent shows and recording as a background singer, I was only singing at school or in the choir. However, my music teacher saw something in me that I didn't.

I sang at school in the vocal ensemble (choir). I was also chosen to sing in this one select group that our music teacher, Miss Henry, would choose for special occasions when the school didn't need the whole choir, just a small group. She chose students in her classes to be in that ensemble, including me.

I loved singing in high school. One day Miss Henry said to me, "I'm proud of you, Rosa, but one day you will really make me proud of you." Having no idea what she was talking about, I said, "How will I do that?" And she answered, "With your voice, of course." I didn't catch on to what she was intimating. "Well, I sing in church," I answered, and Miss Henry said, "No, Rosa. I can see it, and your mom can see it. You can't see it's so because singing professionally doesn't really interest you right now."

If I had to sing, I sang. That was my attitude—at least until the day Barbara, my cousin Joan Marie Johnson, and I formed the Meltones, which became the Dixie Cups, the first successful girl group in the rock era from New Orleans.

So, how did we three teenage girls from the Big Easy end up in the Big Apple and become overnight singing sensations? That mostly has to do with two ambient factors. First was Barbara's ambition and drive, and the second was the rhythm and blues and rock 'n' roll hothouse of talent that enveloped us growing up in New Orleans. Although my sister would prefer to appear only at this book's edges, I do need to talk about her at length in regard to the prehistory of the Dixie Cups.

Barbara was three years ahead of me, so we were never in the same school at the same time. She was already an active participant in school activities while I was in elementary and junior high school. Barbara was also a cheerleader, and at the time, on any given Sunday, high school and junior high school cheerleaders in New Orleans would be invited to one of the local radio stations to perform a cheer for their school. So Barbara and the other cheerleaders would whoop it up for good ol' Carter G. Woodson Junior High School. They would make a day of it, go to the radio station, ride the streetcar from one end of the city to the other, stop for ice cream, and finally go home. If anyone was listening to the radio on Sunday, they might have heard Barbara's name on the radio for the first time.

A little later, something else very fortunate happened to her. One day in high school, Barbara saw two students, Eula Lee Barnes and Barbara Phillips, waiting for her as she was changing classes. Barbara and I had been singing in church with our mother for many years, so if anyone had happened to be there when we were performing, they would know Barbara could do wonderful things to a melody. Eula Lee stepped out and asked Barbara if she could sing a particular tune, which she hummed. Barbara said, "Of course," and Eula Lee asked her to sing it three times. The first time she sang the lines from the unknown song, she did it by herself, and for the next two rounds Eula Lee and Barbara P. came in. That worked out so well, they said to Barbara, "OK, you're in the group." "Er, what group?" Barbara asked, and Eula Lee explained that they were going to compete at the high school talent show, Wa-Lo-Co.

Both Barbara and I attended Walter Louis Cohen. Once a year the city of New Orleans hosted a citywide talent show, and students from all over the city could audition. The song Eula had chosen for the group to sing was "Sugah Wooga," an obscure doo-wop tune recorded on the Savoy label by the Three Playmates. What made it different was that the Three Playmates were the rare female doo-wop singers, which made the song perfect for Barbara, Eula, and Barbara P. The song has a beautiful, humming, "wo-wo-wo" beginning, before the singers launch into, in unison, "Well baby, doncha think maybe / well baby, get along with me / Umm honey, you laughin' like it's funny / umm honey, take a chance with me." Sounds naively romantic, but the structure was more complex, with a forward lead and revolving background. The judges liked it so much the trio won the first-place trophy.

This would have been around 1958 or 1959, which was about the time New Orleans musician and record producer Harold Battiste was first hitting success, arranging "You Send Me" for Sam Cooke. Harold was in California at the time working with Bumps Blackwell, but he came back to New Orleans to do some recording and needed a female back-up singer. I don't think he knew Barbara, but if he asked around, people knew of her and knew she could sing. So he called and asked Barbara to come to this local studio in New Orleans. When Barbara arrived, she realized the other backup singers were men. She would be the only female.

Barbara took music a different way than I did, probably because of her success at the Wa-Lo-Co show. I can't even say I was intrigued by what Barbara was doing. I had my eye on finishing high school, going to college, and becoming a physical education teacher. I never sang outside of school and church while in high school. Barbara did because she hung in a different crowd, which included Athelgra Neville, sister to the more famous Neville Brothers.

Barbara and Athelgra were friends since forever. They were close through high school and continued to be friends after starting college. Barbara and I used to go uptown to the Nevilles' home all the time. Mommee (the name the Neville children and everyone else called Mrs. Neville) considered Barbara and me another set of her daughters. We went on picnics with the Nevilles and enjoyed being together with them on many different occasions. They were good friends with tenor saxman Alvin "Red" Tyler, who at one time had been a neighbor.

The Neville Brothers are like our big brothers. When Aaron had his first regional success with the song "Over You" in 1960, I was just as excited as any of his family. In fact, I didn't look at "Over You" as his first hit, because I just remember that Aaron was well known before he became big, as he had this incredible voice. It seemed he was always recording, releasing records, getting played on the radio. I was proud of my big brother.

The odd thing is that we never worked with Aaron, just with Art Neville. After school Barbara would go to the Neville house and hang out into the evening. Art, Aaron, or their father would bring Barbara back home. Art was always playing the piano, and if she was at the house, Barbara would sing along with him. Later, the Meltones (the original name of the Dixie Cups, when we were performing in New Orleans as teenagers) would sing with Art on his French Quarter gigs.

Art found his place in the local music scene because of Harold Battiste. In 1957 Battiste was working for Specialty Records in Los Angeles, but the owner, Art Rupe, decided he wanted to tap into the New Orleans talent pool and opened an office at 1463 N. Claiborne, above Houston's for Music, a music store owned by William Houston, who was president of the black American Federation of Musicians Local 1496. Rupe hired Harold to manage the new office, which remained open for two years.

Art Neville wrote in the biography *The Brothers Neville:*

> I was just beginning to have a sound of my own. Larry [singer Larry Williams who cut rock 'n' roll standards "Short Fat Fannie" and "Bony Moronie"] introduced me to Harold Battiste, who had just opened a New Orleans office for Specialty Records over on North Claiborne. Harold was incredible, a jazz musician with a feel for righteous rhythm and blues. He helped me put together some demos for label owner Art Rupe and Rupe's main music man, Bumps Blackwell.... A funky white boy who hung around Harold called Mac Rebennack—you know him as Dr. John—wrote something called "What's Going On" that I cut about the same time.

There was a whole group of New Orleans musicians who kicked off the rock 'n' roll era in the late 1940s to mid-1950s, but by the time Barbara and I became teenagers at the end of the 1950s and beginning of the 1960s, there was already a second wave of young singers, our contemporaries, who would become famous, besides Aaron Neville, Art Neville, and the Neville Brothers. I'll mention a few of the performers.

Just by age difference, Barbara was far more involved in the New Orleans music community than I was. She met Willie Tee after he performed at a local show. After a short tenure at Specialty Records in New Orleans, Harold Battiste established the first Black musician-owned record label in the South, called AFO Records. When Willie was about eighteen years old, he began cutting records at AFO Records. It just took time for him to happen, as he didn't have his first hit until 1965, when he recorded "Teasin' You."

Although King Floyd was born in New Orleans the same year as I, it was Barbara who met him at an ILA (International Longshoremen's Association) Labor Union Hall show. When King Floyd was just sixteen, he got his first job at the Sho-Bar on Bourbon Street, in 1961. He was eventually drafted, and afterward he ended up on the West Coast, where he hooked up with an old friend from

New Orleans, Harold Battiste, who arranged King's first album. Another New Orleans music alumnus King met in Los Angeles was Mac Rebennack (Dr. John), who cowrote some songs with King for that first album. King's big break came in 1970 when he met still another New Orleans musician on the West Coast, Wardell Quezergue. Known in New Orleans as the Creole Beethoven, Wardell convinced King to come back to the South and record with Malaco Records in Jackson, Mississippi. Also in the recording studio that day was Jean Knight, who was working on a song called "Mr. Big Stuff." For that session, King sang an old song of his, "Groove Me." It broke first in New Orleans and then went on to become a #1 hit on R&B charts and a Top 10 record on the *Billboard* Hot 100. It was a million-seller and certified gold record.

After we were established as the Dixie Cups, we met fellow New Orleans singer Lee Dorsey, who in 1961 had a Top 10 hit record with "Ya Ya." What's interesting about "Ya Ya" is that Lee heard New Orleans schoolchildren chanting the syllables and was able to take the raw New Orleans patois and transform it into a pop song. It was really not much different from the Dixie Cups taking a childhood memory of a local chant and turning it into "Iko Iko." Indeed, if you put the two song titles next to each other, both are essentially a sound repeated.

Aaron Neville's first successful record, "Over You," was recorded on the local Minit label just prior to Ernie K-Doe coming there to record a novelty rhythm and blues song called "Mother-in-Law," which shot all the way to #1 on the record charts in the spring of 1961. One of the founders of Minit Records was a local disc jockey named Larry McKinley. I believe he also managed Ernie K-Doe for a while. I used to babysit Larry's three children. One time, when I was about sixteen years old, Larry was bringing me home from my babysitting duties and said he had to stop by Ernie's house and bring him some papers to sign. He asked me if I wanted to meet Ernie. "Mother-in-Law" was already popular on the radio stations, so I was excited to actually meet a star. When we got to his house, Ernie's wife answered the door and took us through the residence to his office. On the walk, the one thing that caught my eye was the indoor swimming pool of a striking aquamarine color. That was a lot more impressive than meeting Ernie, who looked shorter than me—and I stood just under five feet, eight inches. He was, however, really pleasant to me. He said in a very friendly manner, "I hope to meet you on a gig sometime." I wasn't sure how to respond beyond a thank-you and ended up saying something formal like that our manager was handling our bookings.

When I was young, the music world in New Orleans took a major turn to rhythm and blues. David Bartholomew found an old song called "Junker's Blues" and rewrote it as "The Fat Man" for robust singer Antoine "Fats" Domino. In December 1949 Bartholomew, Domino, and a bunch of stellar New Orleans musicians (Earl Palmer on drums, Frank Fields on bass, and horn player Alvin "Red" Tyler, among others) headed over to J&M Recording Studio to record "The Fat Man," which became the first major hit for Fats Domino, and what some say was the first rhythm and blues record to connect with white teenagers—a half decade before the likes of Chuck Berry and Little Richard.

By the end of the 1950s, Fats Domino was king of New Orleans rock 'n' roll. He still lived in the city and his affairs were managed by his brother-in-law Reggie Hall. Although we passed by his home many times, we never formally met him until we did a boat show together on the Mississippi River. This happened later on in our career. During my high school years, Fats was past his greatest-hits era of "Blueberry Hill," "Ain't That a Shame," "Blue Monday," etc. Yet he was still making really fine records such as "Walking to New Orleans," "I Hear You Knockin'," and "Jambalaya" at the turn of the new decade.

I never saw Fats Domino in concert. As a teenager I went to only one concert. When I was in high school, I had an uncle who was a policeman and would sometimes get the call to work crowd control or traffic when a performer came to town. I heard that Ike & Tina Turner were coming to town, playing the ILA Labor Union hall for a dance party.

I liked Tina's music, and when I heard that they were coming to New Orleans, I asked my uncle if he was going to be on patrol that night. To my good fortune, he was and he asked if I wanted to see the show. Of course I said yes, but I had to get permission from my mother first. My uncle said, "Let me talk to your mom." He said to her, "Don't worry, I'll have her sit right there on the stage, in a corner, where she can see the whole show and not get into any trouble." I couldn't be out on the dance floor, because the union hall sold liquor. I loved Ike & Tina's whole performance, the way Tina presented herself, the way she worked the audience. She was a very attractive woman. After they finished, Tina walked off the stage in my direction. She stopped and took my hand and said, "Hi, pretty girl." What could I do? I was tongue-tied and just muttered in return, "Hi." When the show was over, my uncle had a patrolman drive me home. As far as I was concerned, that was my first real brush with fame.

I didn't meet any of the other legendary New Orleans musicians, such as Allen Toussaint or David Bartholomew until later, when the Dixie Cups became famous. Meanwhile, Art Neville, who began recording with Harold Battiste and Specialty, switched over to Toussaint's label, Minit, where his brother Aaron had recorded. Toussaint wrote a ballad called "All These Things," which Art recorded. He recalls that session:

> I sang it from the heart, and miracle of miracles, the thing hit big on a subsidiary label called Instant. "All These Things" became Number One in New Orleans.

You'd think that would mean some money for me. At least, I was thinking that way. Well, I was thinking wrong. The truth is that I didn't see a cent in royalties. I had to get a day job. While "All These Things" was being played all over town, I was running an elevator at Gaucho's [Godchaux's], an upscale department store on Canal Street.

After the Meltones traveled to New York for our first recording session, we returned once again to New Orleans. At the time, Art, whom we used to called Artie, was gigging in the French Quarter, playing piano bars, and needed back-up singers, so we joined him. We were all so young we had to enter the club through the back door, which worked out fine, because the piano was behind the bar and was the only place we could stand.

Art had a terrific band called the Hawketts, which had an amazing sound that was over-the-top horn based with a trombone, two trumpets, and tenor- and alto-sax players. Later in life, when Art wrote about the Hawketts, this is what he had to say.

> A small band with a big-band sound. The other hot local band was the Flamingos led by Allen Toussaint. Allen had Snooks Eaglin on guitar, a blind man who played the best guitar of anyone in the city. We had John Boudreaux on drums and later Leo Morris, who . . . eventually went off with Sam Cooke and Jerry Butler, winding up in New York where he became Idris Muhammad, a big-time jazz musician. In New Orleans The Hawketts were the number one band.

We never performed with the Hawketts. It was a big band with a big sound. The piano bars in the French Quarter were way too small for the Hawketts. So, to enhance his sound beyond him singing at the piano and to dress up his performance with pretty faces for live shows on the weekend, Art asked Barbara to bring in her group, the Meltones. I don't know what other bars in the French Quarter looked like, as I was still too young to legally be in such places. Since we were underage, we couldn't walk in through the front door. The Meltones were backdoor singers. The place did have a dressing room and a ladies room in the back, and Art made sure no one would bother us. Then when he was ready for us, it was up a set of stairs into a small performance space behind the bar. The only comfort for us was a bench to sit on between sets. To sing we gathered around the piano.

Around the end of 1963 or beginning of 1964, we started with Art, and it wasn't a regular gig, more like every Friday or Saturday night. Art would call Barbara and say, "I'm at the piano bar tomorrow night. You guys want to make a few dollars?" We would get together and decide what we were going to wear, because we didn't have matching show clothes at the time. Still, we would try for similar attire, such as all of us dressing in black or all of us in red dresses. Art would pick us up and then lead us through what was always the door to the kitchen.

Barbara is short. Although the oldest, she always looked to be the youngest. A lot of people thought I was older than Barbara because of my height; I had outgrown her. If we went to the movies together with other friends, she would put her hair in two pigtails and buy herself a child's ticket. I was the tallest in the group, and for photos I always hunched, because I was trying to cut my height down. My mom used to tell me, stand up straight, you have the height so use it—but when you are always the last girl in line in high school because of your height, you have a tendency to not want to be that tall. I didn't really appreciate my height until I started modeling. That's when I realized I had the legs, the body, and I could use it. In the group, however, Joan and I deferred to Barbara. She was our leader.

Saint Augustine High School was one of the most prestigious schools for boys in New Orleans. One had to test to gain acceptance, and boys from all over Louisiana would try for the school. While that might seem elitist, the school also had a famous talent show that was open to everyone. One day Barbara was heading to the supermarket and had to walk past Joan Marie Johnson's house. Joan Marie saw Barbara and came down to the street to greet her, as she had something she wanted to talk to her about. Joan Marie, her brother Howard, and a friend named Robert were organizing a combo to compete at the Saint Augustine High School talent show. As a singing group it was imbalanced, needing one more female voice. She asked Barbara if she wanted to be part of it. Barbara of course said yes, but she would have to get permission from our mom. My mother always encouraged us and said yes, because it would be a fun thing for Barbara to do.

The rehearsal was at our house, and Joan Marie informed us that Robert was not going to make it that night, if indeed at all. Joan Marie explained that his mother had become seriously ill, and as the only male in the family, Robert was going to have to drop everything, including school, to take care of his mom and family. Joan Marie asked Barbara, "Now what are we going to do?" Quick as a wink, Barbara answered, "My sister sings bass." Somewhat insulted, I cut in, "I don't sing bass, I sing second alto," which broke up everyone. But a lot of people in the industry still ask who is that with the bass voice? Anyway, that's how I ended up in the talent show.

Howard, Joan Marie's brother, didn't play an instrument. Instead, he was the aggravator of the group, because he used to work on my last nerve ending and he knew it, so he would keep at it over and over again. He would call me tall, lanky, and no-shape. He said I looked like Olive Oyl, Popeye's girlfriend.

We were stuck with each other, three girls and one boy.

The flyer for the competition read: "St. Augustine's Annual City-Wide Talent Show; Sponsored by the Student Council, February 3, 1963; Categories, Vocal Groups, Instrumental Groups, Soloists (vocal and instrumental); Guest Performers, The Astronauts, The Lorets; Master of Ceremonies, Reynold Decon; Prizes, $100 in cash."

Little did we know there was a talent scout in the audience. His name was Joe Jones.

Everybody got to sing just one song. Ours was "Lovey Dovey Pair," an esoteric doo-wop number originally recorded by the Three Playmates on the Savoy label. This selection showcased a mellow slow-dance beat. The lyrics begin immediately at the opening of the song: "I was walking around the park [doo-wop break] / It was very, very dark [doo-wop break] / But of course I didn't care / Because my man was there." We didn't win—or even place or show—but talent scout Joe Jones liked our sound (and probably our looks!) and circled the Meltones on his program. He notched other names as well, and the one person he really wanted to see was another young lady named Barbara Favorite, who sang solo and came in second place.

Joe Jones might have had a real interest in the Meltones, but he didn't know who we were individually or how to get in touch with us. That all happened by accident. Barbara was babysitting for Larry McKinley, one of the biggest disc jockeys in the South. Also, there was Barbara Favorite from the talent contest, so naturally they chatted about the competition. Then Barbara Favorite said this music guy called her and wanted to meet with her at his office at the Musician's Union on South Claiborne Avenue. Barbara Favorite didn't want to go there alone, so she asked my sister if she would go with her. My sister said yes. They got to the Musicians Union, and the music guy wasn't there. Instead he left a note with his home address. My sister and the other Barbara looked at each other, both thinking this seemed dicey. But opportunity is opportunity, and they went anyway. They knocked on the door of a house that looked as if a big wind would take it away at any moment. Joe came out and they introduced themselves. He seemed to know the other Barbara but not my sister, who said her name was also Barbara. They went in the house, and Joe tried to hold a conversation with Barbara Favorite but kept looking at my sister, which was making her uncomfortable. Finally, he asked, "You were in the group with the girls in the green dresses?" My sister answered yes. And he said, "I thought so. Let me show you something." He went and pulled out his copy of the program and showed my sister he'd put a star and a circle around our name. He said, "I've been trying to find you all."

"Oh, really," Barbara said. "Why?"

"You all were fabulous, and I would like to talk to you about recording."

My sister didn't know who he was. She had never heard of him, didn't know he once had a hit record. Suspiciously she answered, "Oh really. Just when do you think that could happen?"

"Well, when do you think we can get together to talk about it?"

"When you finish with Barbara Favorite."

He went on talking with Barbara Favorite and set up a time to meet with her again. Then he turned to my sister. "I would also like to find another group, the Five Deejays, who performed at the talent show."

"Uh huh, I can help."

"When do you think that could happen?"

"I'm sure they are at my house rehearsing right now."

"Can I come to your house?"

"I have to check with my mom and find out if it's OK." So Barbara called my mom and told her what was going on, and my mom said it would be fine if he came over.

Barbara took a look at the talent show program again and saw Joe had also circled the Five Deejays. They were our friends and often came by to rehearse with us. So, Barbara reiterated, "They are at my house, too," and Joe got very excited.

This meeting took place on a Friday, and when Joe said he wanted to meet the groups, Barbara said, that's no problem because Friday night at the Hawkins house was our usual gathering. On those evenings there would be scary movies on the television, and everyone would come over to watch, eat popcorn, and drink Kool-Aid. Before the show started, the teenagers would sing songs—and sometimes we would even create songs. We had no idea what we were doing, but Joan Marie would write down lyrics, and we would create the melodies.

Joe accompanied Barbara to our house, and when he entered, his eyes grew wide seeing us all in one place. After introductions, he said to Barbara, "I'd like your group to sing a song for me," which we did. Then he asked the Five Deejays to sing. And they did also. After that he asked my mom if he could use the phone. Back then we had a home line and paid separate, high fees for long-distance calls. He didn't ask to make a long-distance call, just to use the phone. My mom, being a good-hearted person, said yes. We didn't stand there to see how many numbers he dialed or who he talked to. We came to find out afterward, he had called Sylvia (Vanderpool) of Mickey & Sylvia fame in New York, and two to four other people, all long distance (expensive calls back in the

1960s). He didn't tell my mom anything. We didn't find out until the phone bill came in that he had taken advantage of our hospitality. He had rung up over $300 on long-distance calls and wasn't man enough to explain to my mother what he was doing.

He told Sylvia, "I have a gold mine here, but I don't have the money to get them to New York. If you send me the money to get them to there, I'll give you half of my manager's fee." We hadn't signed anything yet. This was all in his head. He was conniving and persuasive. Sylvia said yes.

After meeting Joe, the Meltones ended up to be just the three girls. The girl group was what was happening at the time, and Joe realized it would be easier if Howard was not a part of the whole. A straight girl group would be more attractive to record companies. Howard was all right with that and said he was just glad for all his sisters, including Barbara and me.

Joe knew the charts. Coming out of 1963, there were three ways to go for female singers: a solo act such as Skeeter Davis ("The End of the World," #3 top record in 1963), a boy/girl duo like Paul and Paula ("Hey Paula," the #7 record for all of 1963), or befitting our circumstance, as a group such as the Chiffons ("He's So Fine," the #5 record that year).

Our mother had Joe checked out and learned that a few years back he'd had a big hit record. She called uncles, friends, and the musicians she knew to find out anything about this Joe Jones. She was told he had been around the industry a long time and was a talented singer and musician, but her sources also told her that we should be careful, hinting that he was very shady. Our mother weighed all the pros and cons and decided to let us have a shot at making it.

CHAPTER TWO

You Talk Too Much

Joseph Charles Jones, better known to music historians as Joe Jones, accomplished a couple of fine things in his life. In 1960 his rendition of the novelty rhythm and blues song "You Talk Too Much" almost made it to the very top of the charts and finally nestled in as the #3 best-selling song in the country, according to the *Billboard* magazine record charts. Four years later, while attending a talent show in his hometown of New Orleans, he discovered three young ladies who eventually became the singing group the Dixie Cups. Those three Crescent City nightingales tapped for stardom by Joe were Joan Marie Johnson, Barbara Ann Hawkins, and me, Rosa Lee Hawkins, younger sister to Barbara Ann.

Joe seemed to be a talented man who knew the music business, and that attracted many an up-and-coming performer. Unfortunately for anyone who fell into his orbit, the truth was very different from the facade. In reality, Joe was an awful excuse for a human being. He was greedy, exploitive, angry, untruthful, and manipulative, and he was a rapist. In short, he was a mean S.O.B., and to this day I have disgust for him because of what he did to the Dixie Cups—and what he did to me personally. I have nothing but contempt for him. I won't use the word *hate*, as I don't want to bring that negative energy into my life. But if he had used and abused you physically and mentally, if he had cheated you in business, you would have the same opinion of Joe Jones as I have.

Like all of us, Joe grew up in New Orleans. A researcher found census records from 1940 that showed his father was named Charles and was a warehouseman at a place called the Wholesale Fur Company. His mother was named Alice. She was 62 at the time of the census, and Charles was 58. They had three children in a row, the oldest, Annabell, was 15; Joseph, 14; and Bernadine, 13. Charles and Alice were no youngsters when she started having children, so they appeared to be in a hurry to get all that birthing out of the way. Joe was born August 12, 1926.

It's hard to say when the lying started for Joe, but it would reach back to his teenage New Orleans years. Men born in the mid-to-late 1920s were too young to serve in the military at the start of World War II, although many of the older boys would become of age before the war ended. After the United States entered the war, in December 1941, the Selective Service Act required that all men between the ages of eighteen and sixty-five register for the draft. So between November 1940 and October 1946, over ten million American men were registered, including Joe. Many of the men born in 1926 and later were drafted or enlisted but never fought in the war. However, as they got older, the stories they told would be much more heroic than that, often mentioning their daring deeds in World War II, a conflict they actually missed. Somewhere along the way, Joe began to fudge his military service experience, so you can find in an obituary (Joe died in 2005, following quadruple bypass surgery) or online that Joe enlisted at age sixteen or that he served in the navy during World War II. None of this is true.

My researcher discovered a copy of Joe's military registration card. He was living at 2114 New Orleans Street in New Orleans, unemployed and nineteen years old, as of August 12, 1945. At that point, Joe had not yet been drafted or enlisted, and World War II officially ended on September 2, 1945.

Joe always said to us he served in the navy, enjoyed being in the service, and was able to travel all over the world. Being in the navy meant he would have enlisted and served for four years. By one account he played piano in a military band, which would have made sense, as Joe was a good pianist.

Since Joe was a habitual liar, most official biographies go off track somewhere about this moment on his timeline. If he enlisted right after his nineteenth birthday, he would have served into 1949. Again, according to Joe, he was in New Orleans at the end of the 1940s with his own band, the Atomic Rebops. Joe would also tell anyone who would listen that after his stint in the navy, he didn't go immediately back to New Orleans but went to New York, where he studied at the Juilliard Conservatory of Music. Even if that was remotely true, enrollment at the prestigious Juilliard would have been for a nanosecond. After four years in the service, Joe would have been in his early twenties and anxious not to be a student but cutting his way in the world of popular music, and there were few better places to be at the end of the 1940s than in New Orleans.

Other Joe stories indicate he was in New Orleans at the end of the 1940s after his military service. Some people put Joe in New Orleans in 1947 because he boasted that members of his band, and he himself, played on Roy Brown's seminal, pre-rock 'n' roller, "Good Rockin' Tonight." Again, if Joe was in the navy, he wouldn't have been back in New Orleans until, at earliest, 1949, although the band he put together could have included musicians who had played on the recording, which some people call the first rock 'n' roll record.

Roy Brown was a Louisiana boy, born and raised in small towns before his family moved to Houston, where he went to high school. He started out as a crooner, moving to the West Coast and then back to Texas, where he wrote "Good Rockin' Tonight" for his own band. Since he preferred to croon, he let another band member sing the harder, bluesier "Good Rockin' Tonight," until the night that band member didn't show up for a gig and Roy took on his own song. Roy liked it so much that he went to New Orleans to offer it to blues singer Wynonie Harris, who turned him down. So he then took it to singer Cecil Gant, who had him sing it over the telephone to Julius Braun of De Luxe Records in New Jersey. As author Larry Birnbaum writes, when Braun came down to New Orleans in early summer 1947 for a Paul Gayten recording session at J&M Recording Studio, he stayed around long enough also to record Roy Brown singing "Good Rockin' Tonight." The backup group was drummer Bob Ogden's combo, sometimes referred to as the Bob Ogden Orchestra or the Bob Ogden Band.

Here's the way writer Jeff Hannusch lays out the players:

> Immediately after the session, Braun took his masters back to Linden, New Jersey. Roy was hired by Ogden to sing down at the Black Diamond Restaurant on North Galvez and Conti Streets, along with Sporty Johnson, Myrtle Jones and Alma Parnell. By May, Good Rockin' Tonight was released, and the entire revue moved on to the more prestigious Robin Hood club, on Jackson Avenue and Loyola.

Just taking into consideration the Bob Ogden group's name discrepancy, the backup musicians to the song could have been a handful of Bob Ogden regulars or an expanded group, and anyone of them might have ended up with the Atomic Rebops. The only person surely not there was Joe Jones, and there were no Atomic Rebops in 1947.

If you search hard enough on the internet, you might find an amplified obituary of Joe Jones, including this comment: "He formed the band Joe Jones and his Atomic Rebops, the first of many that he would lead, employing a pool of New Orleans musicians including Melvin Lastie, Lee Allen and Harold Battiste, all of whom would go on to carve out substantial careers."

Little of that statement is true.

Lastie is a prominent family name of musicians in New Orleans. Melvin was a horn player born in 1930. I didn't know him or the other Lasties, such as saxophonist David or drummer Joe. As for Lee Allen, who is a legendary New Orleans sax player, in 1947 he was playing with the Paul Gayten Band and later with Dave Bartholomew. Writer Ed Ward has him in the early 1950s with the Fats Domino band and in the studio at Little Richard's first recording session. When interviewed for *I Hear You Knockin': The Sound of New Orleans Rhythm and Blues*, Lee Allen recalled forming the studio band with Bartholomew that worked out of J&M Studio during the early 1950s with guys like Earl Palmer on the drums, Frank Fields on bass, and Alvin "Red" Tyler on tenor sax. Never a mention of Joe Jones. Lee had a big instrumental hit in 1958 with "Walking with Mr. Lee."

While Harold Battiste, a real New Orleans legend, was never in a band with Joe Jones (born in 1931, he was a student either in high school or at Dillard University, where he earned a bachelor of science in music in 1953), he is somewhat responsible for the existence of the recording star Joe Jones. He was the producer/arranger on Joe's one big hit, "You Talk Too Much."

New Orleans is well known as a jazz town, but it is less well known as a place where rhythm and blues percolated up from down-home musicians to create the music that has swept the world since the mid-1950s. In fact, New Orleans has been a rhythm and blues city since the late 1940s and should get some consideration as the birthplace of modern American music, because it was the meeting of country, blues, and rhythm and blues that served as the foundation for rock 'n' roll.

In 1947 two musicians who were born elsewhere relocated to New Orleans to record some soulful R&B tunes. Paul Gayten, a Californian, recorded the song "True," an update of Don Albert's 1936 ballad "You Don't Love Me," which music writer Larry Birnbaum tabs as the first national R&B hit by a New Orleans artist. There Paul met Annie Laurie from Atlanta, who with Gayten at the piano recorded "Since I Fell for You" at the local J&M Recording Studio owned by Cosimo Matassa. Most people know only the version by Lenny Welch, which was a monster hit in 1963—and the version that I knew well.

Although the musical community was outsized, New Orleans in the 1950s and early 1960s wasn't that large a city by population, and most musicians knew one another or at minimum knew of each other. So when Joe Jones came to our house, tossing up his big pitch about making Barbara, Joan Marie, and me recording stars, he also came with some background. Somehow I didn't remember the song "You Talk Too Much," but my mother had heard of it. She didn't know who recorded it, so when Joe Jones appeared, he was a stranger. Like a good mom, she asked around, finding out he was a bona fide recording star. On the downside, there were also negative comments that Joe was somewhat of a shady character.

He admitted to being expelled from the local chapter of the American Federation of Musicians. Joe's story was that he had been attempting to set up a rival organization. The trouble with that tale was that there were already two unions in town. As with other big cities that attracted many Black musicians, such as Kansas City, the local branch of the AFM didn't admit Black players, so they had to form their own union. In New Orleans, the two separated and segregated unions wouldn't merge until the 1970s. Joe, if he was expelled, would have faced the music, so to speak, from what was called at the time the Negro Musicians' Union. Joe played fast and loose and probably violated basic union rules rather than doing something heroic such as starting another union. While Joe claimed he was reinstated, by 1963 he still wasn't fully trusted by the New Orleans musical community.

As Dr. John told writer John Broven: "He [Joe Jones] talked his way into deals, and talked his way out just as quick. He had big ideas, and although Joe got his feet in the door, he had no talent to stay there."

When you read things that say when Roy Brown came to town to record "Good Rockin' Tonight" and used a "good portion of Jones's band," that's misleading. A more accurate phrasing would be that Jones's band consisted of men who had backed up Roy Brown when he came to town. And Joe's band wasn't around for that long.

In 1948 Lowell Fulson recorded a song called "Three O'Clock Blues." B.B. King, who was a Memphis disc jockey at the time, rerecorded the song in December 1951, and it rose to the #1 position on the rhythm and blues charts. In 1952 "Three O'Clock Blues" was the sixth-best-selling R&B song of the year. King was touring in the South to support the song and came to New Orleans, probably in 1952. Joe had said in interviews that when B.B. King came to New Orleans, he needed a piano player immediately, and Joe sat in. King must have liked him, because Joe joined King's band as a pianist, but also as a driver and valet.

That gig lasted until around 1954, when Joe issued his first single, "Adam Bit the Apple," on Capitol Records. The dates are important because Joe conflated his relationship with New Orleans singers Shirley & Lee (Shirley Goodman and Leonard Lee), who had a huge crossover hit with "Let the Good Times Roll" in 1956. He either discovered Shirley & Lee or backed the duo up at recording, or toured behind them with his band, depending on what one reads about Joe.

Of those options the one statement that's absolutely inaccurate is that he discovered Shirley & Lee, who started recording in 1952 when Joe was going off with B.B. King. Writer Larry Birnbaum, in his book *Before Elvis: The Prehistory of Rock 'n' Roll*, explains: "In 1952, Cosimo Matassa played Eddie [Eddie Mesner of Aladdin Records] a demo tape that a group of teenage singers had paid him two dollars to record. Mesner recruited the lead singers, Shirley Goodman and Leonard Lee, to redo their song 'I'm Gone' for Aladdin that June with Dave Bartholomew's band. . . . 'I'm Gone' was a No. 2 R&B hit for Shirley & Lee."

Birnbaum doesn't say who the background musicians are, other than Lee Allen, which indicates it was Dave Bartholomew's band of regulars at J&M Records.

Around 1957 Joe signed with the small Herald Records in Elizabeth, New Jersey. Never a powerhouse, the small label did sign Lightnin' Hopkins in 1954 and could boast major hits such as "Shake a Hand" by Faye Adams and "Stay" by Maurice Williams & the Zodiacs. Joe wasn't successful at the label, recording one single, "You Done Me Wrong," with "When Your Hair Has Turned to Silver" on the B-side.

Two years later, he ended up on Roulette Records, a New York label founded by a group of tough and "connected" New York characters, including George Goldner and Morris Levy. Although Roulette was considered a front organization for the mob, it was a very successful label from the 1950s through the 1960s, recording Buddy Knox, Jimmie Rodgers, Ronnie Hawkins, and Joey Dee and the Starliters.

Joe recorded a number of singles, including "You Talk Too Much," with Roulette starting around 1958. The tune had an interesting history. In 1958 Reggie Hall wrote the song for his brother-in-law Fats Domino, who decided not to record it. But it was known in New Orleans, where Joe heard it. The song was somewhat goofy; the beginning lyrics went like this: "You talk too much, you worry me to death / You talk too much, you even worry my pets." Nevertheless, Joe, who had been around the music industry for quite some time and had a good feel for pop sensibilities, decided to record the song for Roulette. It's also been said, and I strongly concur, that the song appealed to Joe because it defined him. He could talk you to death, although at the end of any long Joe conversation, the person affected by the wrong end of his gibberish was himself.

The confusion around recording the song "You Talk Too Much" was typical Joe. In 1960 he recorded the song for Roulette, which immediately shelved it. Considering the company's reputation and the men who ran it, Roulette was not a label one should challenge. Nevertheless, Joe, still high on the song, returned to New Orleans, where he recorded it again on the tiny New Orleans label Ric with a better arrangement by Harold Battiste. This was Joe playing fast and loose, because he didn't have the rights to the song. Roulette did and when "You Talk Too Much" started to catch on with deejays, Roulette lowered the boom, filing an injunction against Ric, forcing it to withdraw its version. George Goldner now knew that "You Talk Too Much" had potential, and he probably slid Ric an offer it couldn't refuse, because the song quickly reappeared on the Roulette label, where it went on to fame and fortune, but not for Joe. He made little money from that very successful recording or the straight-to-the-cutout-bin follow-up attempts, "One Big Mouth" in 1960 and "(I've Got a) Uh Uh Wife" in 1961.

As I noted, Joe knew a good pop song when he heard one, and he had one more shot at the fame part of being a recording act. In 1961 Joe recorded an unusual song for an R&B act, "California Sun." Written by Henry Glover, it was a paean to California at a time when southern Blacks were more interested in moving to places like Michigan, where better jobs could be found. A year later the Beach Boys charted for the first time with the song "Surfin'," ushering in the surf music craze of the early 1960s; and a white group, the Rivieras, in 1964 rerecorded "California Sun," replacing background saxophone with a driving organ and highlighting a shrill electric guitar, giving it a surf vibe. Now in tune with the times, the song hit #5 on the *Billboard* charts.

At the same time Joe was failing as a recording star and looking around for other ways to make money in the music world, Barbara, Joan Marie, and I were succeeding despite ourselves. Or, to be more accurate, succeeding despite me, still too young to have aspirations, and so just hanging with Barbara and her friends and having fun.

CHAPTER THREE

Marie Laveau

After Sylvia Vanderpool decided to back Joe's talent scouting venture in New Orleans, it was time for Joe to convince the parents that their children could be recording stars. He began by selling himself, talking about his hit record. My mother, Mrs. Lucille Cordelia Merette Hawkins, immediately cut him off. "What record did you have?" Joe, a little taken aback, because he naturally assumed everyone had heard of him, answered, "You Talk Too Much." I'm not sure if my mother knew the song or not at that very moment.

The first pitch to my mom and Joan Marie's mother wasn't so much that he was going to record us but what he could do for us as singers—the usual overblown promises of our names being plastered all over billboards and crowds of people seeing us at shows. My mother and Joan Marie's mother bought in. Then it was a matter of coming up with the contracts and other legal documents, because I was still considered a minor—and probably Joan as well. My mother had a friend look over the legal papers and contracts, which he said were legitimate.

She would let us go.

My mother, who was very careful, conscientious, and God-fearing in raising Barbara and me, allowed us to go to New York with a music promoter because she herself had been in the music business and left it only so that she could properly raise her two girls. This had been in the heyday of acclaimed New

Orleans bandleader Oscar Phillip Celestin, known to all as Papa Celestin. He essentially had two disjointed careers, before World War II and after World War II. It was during Papa Celestin's second go-round that my mother sang with his group, the Tuxedo Jazz Band.

When he was twenty-six, in 1910, Papa Celestin became leader of the house band at the Tuxedo Dance Hall at the edge of Storyville, the legendary red-light district in New Orleans that birthed a new music in America, jazz. After the dance hall closed, Papa Celestin kept the Tuxedo name for the various iterations of bands he led, eventually settling on the Tuxedo Brass Band. Among the famous that played with Papa Celestin in the early days were trumpeter Louis Armstrong and cornetist Joe Oliver. He recorded with Okeh and Columbia, and all seemed good until the Depression hit, followed by World War II, and Papa left the business to get a steady paycheck at the shipyards.

After the war was over, Papa Celestin created a new Tuxedo Brass Band, which proved even more popular than the first, often performing at the Paddock Lounge on Bourbon Street. As I always say, New Orleans has an outsized reputation for music, but it is not a big city, and musicians of all stripes tend to cross paths.

In *Blue Monday: Fats Domino and the Lost Dawn of Rock 'n' Roll*, Rick Coleman writes:

> After the War, in 1946, [Harrison] Verrett took Fats Domino to his gig with the Original Tuxedo Jazz Band, led by Oscar Papa Celestin.... In the courtyard patio of the French Quarter restaurant The Court of Two Sisters, Domino sat down and played his boogie woogie for white patrons, who deposited change and bills in the tip jar.

Fats Domino wasn't the only early New Orleans rock 'n' roller to play with Papa Celestin. Again, from Rick Coleman:

> By the age of twelve, Dave [Bartholomew] began sitting in with his father's bands. After stints in the bands of Joe Robichaux and Papa Celestin (who took Bartholomew out of the ninth grade to go on his first tour).... one night Sam Cimino... asked Bartholomew if he would form a band to play at a club he was opening in six weeks called the Graystone. With the help of Clarence Hall, a sax player from Papa Celestin's group, Bartholomew put together a band, buying them cheap striped suits.

In the early 1950s, Papa Celestin had the most popular band in New Orleans. Then in 1954, when he was about seventy years of age, he recorded the bayou classic "Marie Laveau." The tale of Marie Laveau is long and winding, with a sad but appropriate ending:

> Marie Laveau had passed away.
> In St. Louis' Cemetery she lays in her tomb,
> She was buried at night on the waste of the moon.

When I was a youngster, my mother, who was very pretty, was already the front singer for Papa Celestin. I can't say when she actually started with him. All I remember was when I was of elementary school age she didn't have a regular nine-to-five job. What happened with her was that she had to stop singing, partly because my grandmother did not believe in the music industry. More importantly, my mother didn't have anyone, besides our grandmother, to keep Barbara and me when she went on a gig, because Papa Celestin was big news around Louisiana and the surrounding states and his band traveled.

Mostly, Papa Celestin played the clubs in New Orleans and my mother was on his schedule. If my grandmother was in a nice mood, she would say to my mother, "I'll keep them for you," and we would go right around the corner to our grandmother's place. Sometimes we would have to stay the whole weekend. If my grandmother was busy, two young ladies from the neighborhood would babysit us.

The real pleasure for me was watching my mother get ready for an evening show. I used to think we were rich because of the fine way she dressed—all of her clothing was beautiful and meticulously cared for. I mean, she used to brush her suede shoes to make the suede sit up. Oh, she had this royal blue dress that I can still picture in my mind today. I used to lie across her bed when she got dressed and put her makeup on at the vanity. She was always so precise. Back then the undergarments you bought in established stores were always black, white, or beige—that was it, the only colors. But my mother had different-colored undergarments to match her dresses, because she would use Ritt to dye undergarments in the washing machine, running it on the soft cycle. My favorite colors were the royal blue, red, and soft pink. When she got dressed to go to church, all the ladies wore black dresses. Sometimes she would say, you have to step out while I put on my undergarments, and then she would call me back in. I would lie there as if in another world. She and I would make earrings, although I didn't like the hanging earrings, because they reminded me of the ladies who worked the night. When I said that to my mother, she looked hard at me and said, "And when did you see those kinds of women?" Growing up in New Orleans, you tended to see a lot of those ladies.

From her time of being the front singer for a big band, I still have one or two pictures of her standing by the piano. I knew about her being a singer, but

I was so young it didn't really mean anything to me at the time. I just knew my mom was a performer and that she sang with a big band. I can't recall exactly when my mother stopped singing. My grandmother had been keeping us, and my mother was under pressure because my grandmother didn't believe the singing was going to put food on the table.

When our chance came along, I was attending Southern University, and I really didn't think she was going to let me drop out to pursue a career, but she said to me, "You succeeded, you graduated from high school, and these opportunities don't come along all the time." She said she wouldn't stand in our way if we wanted to try for a singing career, that we should go ahead and take the shot.

Actually, my mother didn't stop singing. She just switched venues, from nightclubs to the church. This was also where Barbara and I first sang; we were always in church choirs. Often my mother, Barbara, and I would sing as a trio: my mother was first soprano, Barbara sang second soprano, and I sang alto. My mother sang in our first church, which was Saint Mark's. She was in the Pastor's Aid Choir. We stayed with that church through elementary school. Barbara and I often used to walk to the church; we didn't take the bus, because we would go on to Sunday school. I never saw my mother sing outside of church unless someone had a special program going on and they wanted her to perform elsewhere.

If a unique event was going to be organized at the church, they would just come to my mom and say, "Lucille, I would like you and your girls to do a song." Mother would always say OK. We would, as a trio, decide what gospel song we were going to perform, rehearse, and then sing as scheduled. I was glad every time we were asked to be on the programs, as I enjoyed being in front of an audience. Even when young I never had qualms about being on stage. It really was just another part of my life as a child. It wasn't as if we were preparing to go into show business.

My mother's family came from the south-central Louisiana town called Sunset. It was a country town, not very big, fewer than two thousand people.

When we got older, our mother took us to Sunset to see our grandmother, who lived with her brother Joe. Boy, he was a trip, doing tricks and saying crazy things. He always had us laughing. When we visited we had our own room, with a big four-poster bed that Barbara and I shared. My grandmother used make a kind of peach brandy, and one time Uncle Joe knocked at our door. Our grandmother yelled to him, "What are you doing?"

He was carrying a bottle of the homemade liquor. He yelled back, "I'm going to give these girls a taste of Sunset."

"Don't give my babies that rotgut, it will make them sick," Grandmother replied. "They are city girls and don't know anything about homemade liquor."

Uncle Joe came into the room and unscrewed the bottle, and that smell was really nasty. We complained to our grandmother, "Ugh, do we have to drink that?"

Now angry, she said, "Joe, I don't want you to give them that stuff." That worked and Uncle Joe left the room. Grandmother told us, "If Joe comes back and tries to make you drink that, I'll take the broom to him."

Joe, who was a lot older than our grandmother, ran a barber shop that was attached to the house in Sunset. When Grandmother was small, she came into the barber shop and wanted a nickel for ice cream. Joe was sharpening his razor and said no. Grandmother was just a child, and she was going to jump into Joe's lap and beg for that nickel. Just at that moment, Joe had swung around, still holding the razor. He cut her throat from one end to the other. Grandmother screamed. Her mother, our great-grandmother ran into the room. Quickly she tore into the attic, gathered up cobwebs and tobacco from their dad's pipe, put it on the wound and wrapped it with a white towel. Our grandmother wore that for a week. Joe, who thought at first he killed his little sister, always felt guilty. At eighty years old, her scar was barely visible. Our grandmother laughed when she told us that story because, she said, "After that, any time I would ask for a nickel, I would always get it."

The nearest big city was Lafayette. My grandmother used to say, "If you blink your eyes, you're gonna pass it by." One time my grandmother, Mrs. Cordelia Merette, wanted us to visit family in Sunset, so we took the Sunset Limited from New Orleans. We called Mrs. Cordelia Merette our grandmother, because our mother referred to her as our grandmother, but she was really my mother's great-aunt. My mother's real mother was named Bessie Nelson. In a form of interfamily welfare and service, what they used to do if a teenager or very young woman in the family got pregnant and went on to have a baby, one of the elders would take on the responsibility of raising that child. When my mom was born to Bessie, who, at the time, was too overburdened to be an effective parent, she was passed to Cordelia to raise. My mother was Bessie's fourth child. Her first two children had the same father and were named Julia and Bessie. My family doubled down on names all the time, so there was Mama Bessie and Grandma Bessie. If you grew up with them, it all made sense, but when I came along I didn't know who Mama Bessie was or who Grandma Bessie was. (Grandma Bessie's daughter was Mama Bessie.) The third of Bessie's girls was Elnorie, and my mother, Lucille Cordelia Merette, was the last girl. However, there were rumors going around the family that there was a boy somewhere in the mix, but nobody could tell us what the boy's name was or who his dad was.

I have my grandmother's wedding certificate to her husband Ben Nelson. My mother was born in 1923. When Barbara was born, Cordelia Merette, the great-aunt, took in Barbara, and then when mother gave birth to me, her last child, my grandmother took me in as well. She started raising us while Mother was on the road with Papa Celestin.

My mother was born in Sunset, Louisiana. The family moved to New Orleans, and then later to Chicago. Mother didn't like the weather in Chicago and was glad when they moved back to Louisiana. I used to tease her. Any time I saw a Mafia movie, I would kid her. "Ma Dear (I would call my mom "Ma Dear"), were you around when Al Capone was in Chicago?" She would exclaim, "I'm not that old!"

My father was a construction worker named Hartzell Hawkins. He was married before he met my mother, but his wife died in childbirth. She had a girl and named her Shirley, who is our older sister. After graduating from Booker T. Washington High School, Shirley met a guy named Wallace Washington, who worked on the riverfront, which at the time offered the best-paying jobs to Blacks in New Orleans. Shirley and Wallace married and had five boys.

My mother met my father when she came back to New Orleans, and they married soon afterward. They had two girls, Barbara and Rosa. Eventually they separated but never divorced.

I don't know if our ancestors had been slaves, because all the time we were growing up, no one in our family ever mentioned that our ancestors had been slaves. My "grandmother" Mrs. Cordelia Merette told us our grandfather was originally from Morocco. An ancestor, Julian Como (could also be Comeaux or other similar spellings), came to New Orleans in the 1800s and married a woman he called Mary Jane, who was a Choctaw Indian. There are still a lot of people with the name Como (or Comeaux) throughout Sunset and other small towns in the area. In fact, our family owned hundreds of acres of land in the area.

We had cousins in Sunset we didn't get to see very much, and when we went there with our grandmother, they called us city girls. One of the cousins was on the porch and said, "Come here, city girl. I want you to look as far as your eyes can see." I asked, "What am I looking for?" He said, "That's all our land."

We never met our biological grandfather Benjamin Nelson, until he came into New Orleans to have eye surgery. He called my mom and said he wanted to see his two grandkids that he had never seen before. This man was very tall (and my son is tall like him). He also had light brown skin. In New Orleans, due to the long history of racial interrelations, sometimes you can't really tell if the person next to you is white or Black, and he was like that. He was a good-looking man.

At that time, when my grandmother came to New Orleans, she had my mother and her son Ernest with her. She had a second son named Willie, who was in the army during World War II. My grandmother was lucky enough to get into subsidized apartment housing that was known as "the projects." In New Orleans the projects were two-story structures with a minimum of four apartments to a building, two upstairs and two downstairs. At the time, there were more white people in the projects than Black people. That was in 1950, and I was five years old, ready to start kindergarten.

At first, when my mother stopped singing and was ready to make a home for her family, meaning Barbara and me, she could afford only a one-bedroom apartment in Uptown, a neighborhood between the French Quarter and Jefferson Parish. She had the bedroom, and Barbara and I slept on a sofa bed. That lasted only about six months. Then we moved to the Calliope Projects, which were in the second ward, fourth precinct. Our new apartment boasted two bedrooms. Barbara and I had our own bedroom, with twin beds, and my mother had a bedroom. The apartments in Calliope boasted a full bathroom with a large tub and space heater, a major improvement for many who moved there from substandard housing conditions. We had a telephone on what was known as a party line; there were three other families on our party line. My father did not contribute to our rent, so my mother worked, eventually getting a job helping Rev. Avery Alexander, who was influential in Black politics in Louisiana.

It was the first of many steps upward for my mother, who also was the first woman secretary for the NAACP in Louisiana. In 1959 she started her political career, running for the Democratic Party executive committee, but with few resources, she didn't win. Her publicity efforts were a mixed bag. One flyer showed a picture of a young and very pretty woman, with the headline "Elect 109." Then below, in big letters, "Lucille Hawkins," followed by the phrase "Orleans Parish Democratic Executive Committee Ward 2, December 5, 1959."

A photo in the local paper showed a slightly older—but still young—woman with the more formal attribution "Mrs. Lucille M. Hawkins, candidate for Orleans Parish Democratic Exec Com." This was followed by a brief biography: "Attended New Orleans elementary schools and McDonogh 35 High School. Married and the mother of 2 daughters. Active in Church and Civic circles. Secretary, 2nd Ward Voters Assn. Executive Secretary for U.N.I.A. Div. 320, N.O.V.L. & N.O. Civic and Ind. Assn."

The picture in the publication was the same one she used for her columns written for a local newspaper. At the start of 1966, her column was called "For Tots and Teens," but by the middle of the year it was retitled "The World of Youth," with two subheads. The first read, "Schools-Colleges-Scouts-Clubs, and the second read, "Weekly prizes courtesy of People's Life Insurance Company."

She was a very brave soul at a time when segregation in the South was very strong. She took a white man to court for interfering with her right to vote. I was there when the incident happened. At the time the voting booths had little curtains to pull so you could vote in private, with no one seeing who you were voting for. I was with my mom, and I remember her telling me not to touch any of the levers. I didn't need a reminder, as I was shy child and content to hold onto my mother's skirt. Just as she was about to pull the levers to vote, this white man pulled the curtains aside. My mother said, "Sir, I'm still in here." He said in a no-uncertain voice, "No, you're finished. Get out." I looked up at my mom, and she said, "I beg your pardon." Still menacing, he snarled, "You heard me. I said get out, and if you don't get out, I'm going to call the police." As a child, if someone says they are going to call the police on your mom, what do you do? You burst out in tears. When my mother was upset with me or trying to soothe me, she would call me Rosa Lee. At that moment, she said to me, "Now, Rosa Lee, I want you to stop crying, nobody is taking me to jail." My mother stood there. He used the N-word and said, "I want you to get out of here," and Mother opened the other end of the curtain and called out to the man running the polling place, "I need a policeman here." The guy knew my mom and said, "What's the matter, Mrs. Hawkins?" And she said, "This man walked in, opened the curtain, and I hadn't finished." Seeing that my mother hadn't finished the physical act of voting, the menacing white guy pressed the remaining levers, so she took him to court. The incident made the local news. The man claimed my mother had already voted. And the judge asked him, "How could she do that if the poll worker hadn't finished pushing down the final lever to record the votes?" He said, "They must have been working together. All I know is she pushed what was necessary." He said he was assisting Lucille Hawkins, but my mother claimed he changed her votes. This all led to citywide voter fraud hearings.

On Tuesday, June 3, 1958, a local New Orleans paper ran photos of four people across the top of the page. The caption read: "THESE FOUR PERSONS figured in the high spots of today's second session of the vote fraud hearing. Poll commissioner Ted Coppersmith, left, said he merely assisted voter Lucille Hawkins, second from left. She said he changed her vote. Mr. and Mrs. Ulric Vial, right, said they didn't vote, while commissioners insisted they must have."

My mother won the case.

I attended the Sylvania F. Williams Elementary School, which was just for Black children. The teachers and principal were also Black. White families also lived in the Calliope Project, but they went to any other school their parents could get them into.

I started my singing career in the children's choir of Saint Mark's Baptist Church when I was about six years old. I never had a singing lesson. I was just blessed, a gift from God and my mother, to be able to sing. Once, the principal from my elementary school was visiting Saint Mark's and saw me in the choir. When church was over, she called me to her and asked, "Rosa, do you sing?" I said, "Yes, ma'am." She said, "You are going to start singing the national anthem and 'The Sunny Side of the Street' at the school," because the elementary school always had all-school, Monday-morning meetings at the flagpole. Sure enough, she had the teachers call me out. I sang "The Sunny Side of the Street," the next week the national anthem, and the week after something else. It wasn't difficult, as the school had a limited repertoire of songs I had to know. The knowledge that I was a singer would follow me through elementary school and then all the way into high school. Any time we had assembly and the school needed a soloist, they got Rosa Lee Hawkins.

My mother made sure we had a well-rounded life. She took us to many of the museums in New Orleans. We were even introduced to the symphony. She made sure Barbara and I experienced a tea party, which was a significant event for New Orleans women at the time. She was showing her daughters how to be grown-ups, which I didn't realize would be important until much later in life. When I became a model, one of my first fashion shows was at this fancy hotel in New Orleans, the Pontchartrain, which had a tea every Tuesday afternoon. It came back to me, what my mom was pitching us—how to act at important functions, why there were so many glasses on the table and different pieces of silverware, and what were the functions of each. She bought the *Amy Vanderbilt Complete Book of Etiquette*. We had the first edition, and she showed me in that book how tables were to be set. She said to Barbara and me, "You never know where you might end up." Who knew, we could end up having dinner with the mayor of New Orleans or even the president of the United States. I taught these very basic skills at the modeling agencies of John Casablancas and Barbizon. We never did have dinner with a president, but we did meet President Bill Clinton, and he sang "Chapel of Love" to us. My mother had a looking glass and could see things in the future that we couldn't see.

The trouble with that looking glass was that it didn't reflect what would happen to her. My mother was a lioness. Even more than that, she was a Lioness—someone who belonged to the Lioness Club, part of the Lions Clubs International. In 1985 members of the Lioness Club were sitting in a suite at the Superdome to watch the New Orleans Saints play football. The suite belonged to the Lionesses, a group of people who stretched out a hand to the underprivileged. It was an integrated group, and this particular gathering of about twenty-five people that my mother belonged to boasted a handful of white members. I would sometimes accompany my mother to meetings, which at the time were located in a side room at a bowling alley.

Barbara and I were there also watching the game. My mother started to say something, but couldn't get it out because she was laughing. She tried again and again, and each time she only ended up laughing. One of our cousins was in town, and she called over to my mother, "Hey, Lucille, what you doing? Every time you get ready to talk, you start laughing." A friend followed up, "C'mon, Lucille, what are you trying to say, because you got us all here laughing as well." She eventually got control of herself and simply said, "I'm not going to say it."

Barbara and I didn't realize anything was unusual, although my mother tried for several minutes to get control—this was during halftime of the football game. When the game came back, everyone drifted back to watching it. My mother said she had to go to the restroom. I offered to go with her, but she told me, "No, I know where it is." She got up and went. I followed just to make sure everything was OK. After the game, we sat around and then went home.

Well, a few years later, Barbara and I were watching a commercial with Danny Glover, and he did two impromptu scenes. First he started crying, and in the other he started laughing. He commented: "If you have a friend or relative and in the middle of conversation they start crying, pay attention to it. Or if they start laughing, it could be they are having a stroke." Barbara and I looked at each other and said, "If only we knew that back then, we could have rushed her to the hospital."

The next time we saw something unusual, my mother was sitting in the den and waiting for Barbara to bring her to work. By this time she worked for the State of Louisiana, at the office of the registrar for voting. She was the first Black woman to hold such a position with the state. Barbara came in my room and said, "Mother is in the den. Go walk up to her and ask her a question and look at her face." I thought, "Oh my God, what?" I decided to take a lighthearted approach.

"OK, Lucille, what's going on?"

She looked at me and said, "I don't know."

I asked, "You know who I am?"

"You're my baby."

"What's my name?"

"Rosa Lee."

I was looking at her face, but I couldn't see anything was wrong.

She said to me, "When is that girl going to be ready to bring me to work? I'm going to be late." She used to call Barbara "that girl."

When I saw Barbara, I told her, "I didn't hear anything wrong, but to me it looked like her face was drawn to one side."

Her job was to give people the application to register to vote and swear them in. She was what was called a Register I. When she started, she was a Register

II, which was a clerical job, meaning she could give the potential voter an application and then pass the completed application to the next person higher on the clerical chart. She worked for a long time and finally became a Register I, which gave her power to swear people into the electorate.

Then bad things started to happen. Her immediate supervisor, who was Black, decided he wanted to have a personal relationship with her. My mother was not going to have any of that and told him so. Yet he kept asking her, saying, "Let me take you to dinner," and "Let's go get a couple of drinks." She didn't equivocate and continued to tell him, "No, no, no, I don't do that."

Out of frustration and anger, he had my mother transferred from the main office to a small district office at a firehouse. It was about three blocks from our house. Usually she would walk. If she didn't feel like walking, she would ask my sister to bring her.

Mother got to work that morning, and this white guy came in to register to vote. My mom gave him the form, which he filled out. She said, "OK, I have to swear you in." After she told him to raise his right hand, all words evaded her. She indicated to the man to please just wait a minute while she took a moment to regain her composure. She tried again but this time she couldn't even say the first couple of words. This man, who was a good person, saw something was very wrong with my mother. He went into the main room of the firehouse and called to some of the firemen, reporting something was wrong with the lady out here, that she was trying to swear him in and she couldn't say the words. The fireman in the station went to my mom and asked what was the matter. As best she could, she responded, "I can't swear him in," and started crying. They brought my mom in the chief's car to the hospital and then called our house. We told the hospital her primary care physician was Dr. Joseph Brenner, who would meet us there. Dr. Brenner, after talking to the emergency room, said to us, "I think your mom had a stroke, and I'm going to be running some tests on her."

Dr. Joseph Brenner, an internist, was a graduate of the University of Pittsburgh School of Medicine, and he came to New Orleans in 1967 to serve as a Lieutenant Commander in the United States Public Health Service, finishing his residency at the Tulane University School of Medicine in the same city. My mom was his first patient out of medical school. By the time he first met Barbara and me, he said, "Your mom talked about you so much. I'm finally glad to meet you." He was more than just a doctor to her; he was a friend to the family. We could call him at home.

We told him about that Lioness Club event in 1985, and he asked why we didn't bring her in then. We said we just didn't understand the signs, that we had never faced anyone having a stroke before and that no on one in our family had ever had a stroke. After listening to our story, he too concluded she was probably having a stroke that time she couldn't control her laughter.

Our mother was admitted to the hospital for further tests. For a couple of days, all seemed normal again. She didn't have another stroke, and she knew who her children were. Tests verified a stroke, but with her being stable, we took her home.

Her health remained steady until July 16, 1999, the day John F. Kennedy Jr.'s plane went down, and I remember that so well because of something she said to me. When she would sit in our den, I sometimes sat with her. Her gaze was turned away from the television, but she could hear the announcer. When the commentary said John F. Kennedy Jr. and his wife, Carolyn, were in the plane that crashed in the Atlantic Ocean off the coast of Martha's Vineyard, she turned around and said, "I'm so sorry. At least he's with his parents." I looked at her and could tell something wasn't right. I told her to turn her head to the left. She turned her head left, but the eyes stayed to the right. I got my sister and told her I thought our mother might be having another stroke. This one wiped her out and removed a lot of her memory. It physically affected the left side of her body. She stayed in the hospital longer and didn't want to eat anymore. The doctor said, "She is not eating because her swallowing muscles are not working." The nurse said, "We can't have her eating anything right now because it would not go down her esophagus and would strangle her." The doctor said he would have to put a tube in her.

The nurse assistant came in, but he just didn't know what he was doing. He was working on an elderly woman, saying to us, "I have to get the tube in there." After the second vigorous attempt, I put my hand on top of his hand and said, "Stop." He said, "She has to have this." I said, "I'll talk to Dr. Brenner, and he will tell you what to do next," because I just couldn't stand to see her lying there crying. The nurse was just not being careful. They put the tube directly into her stomach. What happened with that stroke was that it left her in a state of aphasia, and she could no longer form words. My mother was born in 1923. John F. Kennedy Jr. went down in 1999. She was seventy-six.

For a while afterward she seemed to be getting stronger and going to physical and speech therapy. Oddly, she was still technically employed by the state. One of her checks came in and needed to be signed. One of the ladies from the church was visiting mother, and I told the woman, I have this check for her to sign so I can go put it in the bank. She said to me, "Rose, have your mom sign her name before she can sign her check." I looked at her, and said, "What?" She repeated her concern. I gave my mother a piece of paper and a pen and said, "Write your name, I just want to make sure the pen is OK." When I put that pen her hand—she used to have such a beautiful handwriting—she wrote an

"L" on the paper and then she stopped. She couldn't go any further. I said, "The pen must have stopped working." She answered, "I can't make it write." I shook the pen and said let's try again. "Mom, please write your name." Again, all she could do was the "L." She couldn't write Lucille.

She could still walk a little bit. Dr. Brenner wanted her to have home care seven days a week. One morning the nurse took blood from her early, and then later I got a call from Dr. Brenner's office. They wanted to bring her into the hospital, because her numbers were all over the place. When the ambulance came, they put her on a stretcher and wheeled her down the hallway to the front door. I went in the back and got my jacket and purse because I was going to ride with her in the ambulance. Instead, I just got weak, started sweating, and felt like I was going to pass out. One of the EMTs looked at me and said, "I think you're having an anxiety attack. I need you to go and lie down. Let your sister go." Barbara followed the ambulance in her car. I got ready to lie down because I was beginning to feel dizzy. I called Athelgra, who was singing with us, and said, "I'm having an anxiety attack, and Barbara is at the hospital with Mother."

Four hours later, they hadn't got a room for my mother. I called Dr. Brenner. He told me to stay home. About a half hour later, the emergency room nurse called back to say she would have a room ready in fifteen minutes. They finally got her in a room. Dr. Brenner said this would be a hard one for her to come back from. She was there about a week. I got on my knees and cried and prayed. I promised God, "If you send her back to us, I don't care how we get her back. We will take care of her until you are ready for her to come home."

I didn't realize it would be for almost five years. She died in 2003 from another stroke, at the age of eighty.

CHAPTER FOUR

Thank You Mama, Thank You Papa

At the end of 1963, a few months after the Saint Augustine High School talent show, Joan Marie, Barbara, and I jumped into a car heading north to New York. My mom was all right with us going because she knew God was forging a path for us, and we wouldn't do anything that we weren't supposed to do.

The three of us enjoyed each other's company and were very close. We were young, liked to have fun, and absolutely loved to sing and rehearse songs. Since I was the youngest, my sister and Joan Marie would occasionally tease me. And yes, I didn't always like that. In the car, they were forever telling me to move my long legs, so sometimes I would prop them on the back of the front seat. I would whine, "What am I going to do with the rest of my body?" They would respond with something like, "I don't know, but get it off of me."

Joe had organized a caravan of three cars, because, besides the Meltones, he was bringing a couple of other hopefuls, a singer named Vivian Bates and the Five Deejays. He also had members of his band with him. The excitement of going to New York City didn't last long for me. It was a long, drab, cold drive—especially if Joe was driving, because he liked the window open. For me, who still hadn't come to the full realization that we were going to be recording songs like professional singers, the trip could be defined as "Are we there yet? Are we there yet? Are we there yet?"

The first part of the journey was through the Deep South, and this was the first time I ever encountered blatant racism, such as signs saying bathrooms were for "colored women only" or water fountains only for "colored." New Orleans was, of course, part of the South, but it also was a more accepting city in regard to the coexistence of the races. Segregation existed in New Orleans. It was just not so strident and in your face. For example, when you paid your seven cents to get on the bus, whites sat in front and Blacks in the back, but if you were standing, you could stand anywhere on the bus. Several times I boarded the city bus with my arms filled with my high school texts, and a white girl or woman would get up, telling me I could take her seat. When I would tell my mother about these incidents, she would always say I should be grateful, and that these things happened to me because I had a certain look of the eyes, that I didn't look sad or poor but like someone decent and polite who would say thank you for the seat.

My mother strived to keep the oppression of segregation off our backs, that we should not be limited or stigmatized because we were Black. My mother would take us to the circus when Barnum & Bailey would arrive for its annual visit to the municipal auditorium. If you were white, your parents could get tickets to sit on the floor where, if you were a kid, you wanted to be, because clowns would toss things to you such as candy, teddy bears, and all sorts of junk. Black children had to sit in the upstairs. Barbara and I felt the injustice in the seating. My mother's position was, don't let the seating prevent you from enjoying the spectacle. We may not have been able to sit downstairs, but we could still watch the show. Afterward, with friends, we could still talk about the circus. In addition, Barbara and I were allowed to travel to the municipal auditorium during the run of the shows to see the animals, which were kept in tents and behind fences on adjacent streets. The caretakers of the animals were very kind to the local kids. If they saw a bunch of us peeking through the fence, they would open the gates a little more so we could get a better view. Mostly, we got to see the elephants and the mess they would leave in their wakes. I didn't like to get too close, because those animals stank.

My mother's objective for her children was that we shouldn't miss anything in life that was worthwhile even if we had to deal with inequities of segregation. That's why she enjoyed taking us to museums, because if you had a ticket, you could go anywhere in the museum.

This doesn't mean we didn't take a stand. Or, I should say, Barbara took a stand because she was older than me and more involved in everything. When we took off for New York, I hadn't officially dropped out of Southern University, the New Orleans campus. Barbara had been at the same university before me.

The original campus of Southern University and A&M College in Baton Rouge was established in 1880, making it one of the country's historically black universities. The New Orleans campus, known as Southern University at New Orleans, was created in 1956. Both campuses were strongly involved in the various movements to end segregation. In 1972 two Southern University students were killed by shotgun blasts from police during a round of protests and class boycotts.

Barbara's years coincided with the student boycotts and sit-ins that Black college students were initiating all across the South with the aim of integrating commercial establishments. In urban New Orleans, the main shopping district was along Canal Street, and although 40 percent of the city's population was Black, city laws allowed lunch counters to refuse Black customers. In September 1960 Black and white members of the New Orleans chapter of the Congress of Racial Equality staged a sit-in at the Woolworth's lunch counter. They were arrested. This happened during Barbara's sophomore year, and an ad hoc group of Southern University New Orleans students met with an intent to support the sit-in, so they marched from campus to the Woolworth's. Barbara was walking and chanting along with Athelgra Neville during the march when the police stopped the students, saying they didn't have a permit to march. The students proceeded and were arrested, including Barbara and Athelgra.

When my mom heard about the student march and the arrests on the TV, she exclaimed, "I know that girl is there. I know she is there."

I turned to my mom and said, "Who you talking about?"

She said, "Your sister."

Always tearful me, I started crying.

"What are you crying for?"

"My sister is going to jail, and she didn't do anything."

"Rosa Lee, your sister is not going to jail, and if she is going to jail, we will get her out."

My mother was working for Rev. Avery Alexander, and she called him. He said, "I'll come and pick you up. We'll drop Rosa Lee at your mom's, and then we will go down to the jail and get her home."

If you ask Barbara, she'll tell you jail was fun. The police didn't lock the cells. There was access to the telephone. Basically, the students played cards and waited for parents to come and get them out. The only oddity was a slight mix-up with Barbara. My sister formally signed in as Barbara Ann Hawkins. When they called for Barbara Hawkins, another girl with that name got up, walked to the front, and didn't come back. Little by little, kids left with parents, lawyers, or ministers. Barbara was wondering where our mom was. Reverend Alexander was at the police station with my mother and Athelgra's mom. When they came for Barbara, one of the police said, "We already let her go. What she doing back here?" So they got Barbara and asked, "What is your name," and she said Barbara Ann Hawkins. That's when they realized there were two students with the same name. All the protesting students got suspended from Southern University, because they left the campus without a permit. Most of the students from that year did not return; Barbara didn't go back to Southern.

A couple of years later, we were heading to New York. Barbara was realizing a dream. I was still a naive teenager who had not wrapped her head around the importance of what we were doing. Instead I was trying to put up with a long journey. Joe Jones did not want to spend any extra time on the road, especially in the South, and the caravan hurried north. We stopped to eat but not to sleep in hotels.

When we got to New York, Joe drove straight to Brooklyn, where we met Sylvia Vanderpool, who, after marrying Joseph Robinson, would change her professional name to Sylvia Robinson. She was attractive, talented, and a real go-getter. She would become everything Joe Jones wanted to be but never worked hard enough to become. The successful duo of Mickey & Sylvia, who sang the fiery hit record "Love Is Strange" in 1957, broke up in 1959 but came back together in 1961 to give it another go. It didn't work out, and the year I met her, Sylvia's singing partner Mickey Baker moved to Europe. Sylvia at that point was working on the edges of the music business, trying to find a new gig, so she was receptive to what Joe was offering in regard to new talent coming up from New Orleans.

About two years later, she and her husband moved to New Jersey, where they started their own record label, All Platinum Records, with Sylvia writing songs and coproducing major records such as "Love on a Two-Way Street" by the Moments. As the singly named Sylvia, she had a major hit of her own with a song called "Pillow Talk." If all that wasn't enough, in the 1970s she and her husband, Joseph, would create Sugar Hill Records, which produced the seminal rap record "Rapper's Delight" by the Sugar Hill Gang, which helped mainstream the new music genre.

In 1964 Sylvia was betwixt and between in the music business, so she took a chance on financing Joe Jones's discoveries, including the Meltones. As we drove up to the front of an apartment building, Sylvia came to meet us outside. After all the greetings, we followed her inside, where she sent the Five Deejays to one apartment, the Meltones to another; Vivian Bates would be staying with people she knew. Ours wasn't a big apartment, just one bedroom for the three of us. I bumped into something I had never seen before and said, "Wow, that is hot." It was a radiator, and Sylvia explained, "This is how we get heat in a New York apartment." There was nothing in the refrigerators, so with some of the money our parents gave us, the three of us went shopping. That attracted the Five Deejays, who jokingly asked, "Are you going to cook for us?" We answered sharply, but teasingly, "We're not cooking for you-all."

We were going to be in New York for a limited amount of time, so things had to happen quickly if they were going to happen at all. That first night Sylvia said to all of us, "I will see you tomorrow, as we are going to be pounding the pavement." Huh, what did that mean? She had to be patient with us and our lack of knowledge about New York idioms. Basically, she explained, we would be going to different record companies, trying to get them to listen to us and see if we could get them interested.

At that point, the Meltones had a three-song repertoire, with the most popular of tunes being "Thank You Mama, Thank You Papa." If they asked us to sing a second song, it was "I'm Gonna Get You Yet."

The key lyrics to "Thank You Mama, Thank You Papa" went like this: "Well, I thank you mama and I thank you papa / 'Cause I was 'bout to make a big mistake."

The song was written by popular New Orleans musician and songwriter Earl King, who had played with David Bartholomew and Guitar Slim. His biggest hit was "Always a First Time," a Top 20 record on the R&B charts in 1962. He would write songs for Lee Dorsey. Even Jimi Hendrix would record one of his tunes. But in 1964 Earl gave us "Thank You Mama" to learn for our visits to the record companies. On the record of "Thank You Mama," the songwriter is listed as Ernestine Gaines, which was his pseudonym.

Sylvia's terminology of pounding the pavement was very accurate; we followed Joe into Manhattan, where we would literally walk from one record company to another to another and to another. This was the drill. When Joe walked into a building, he would look at the roster of which companies were tenants. At that time there was usually a display with the company names and on which floors one could find them. Joe would scan it and say, "Oh good, X record company is here." Then we would all trudge to the office, whether it was on the second, fifth, or twelfth floor. If there was a receptionist, Joe would say, "I'm Joe Jones and I have some artists I would like X to listen to." The woman receptionist would ask, "Are you on the schedule?" And Joe would respond, "We just happened to be in the area, and I thought we would stop by." Sometimes that worked and the receptionist would say, "Let me see if Mr. X is available," and sometimes she would say, "Oh, I'm sorry, you have to make an appointment." We got in sometimes, and sometimes not. If we got in, Joe was a great talker, and he would tell Mr. X who he was, mentioning his big record to make sure they knew who he was—not just some bum off the street trying to get recorded. Often, when he said his name, they recognized him. When he mentioned his song, "You Talk Too Much"—who can forget a title such as that?—it rang people's bells. Joe would say, "I have these three young ladies from New Orleans. I found them at a talent show, and I would like you to listen to them." Sometimes we were with the Five Deejays and sometimes not.

If Mr. X wanted to listen to us, we sang "Thank You Mama." Generally, when we sang that song, it was well received. Sometimes, Mr. X would say, "Can we tweak it here, can we tweak it there?" and then we were told to sit out front while Joe and Mr. X did some talking. We would sit looking at each other. At first we were nervous, then not nervous. We would ask ourselves, Is this how it goes? Is this how people make records? We had to keep going, to one place after another. We began to read the nonverbal cues. If Joe came out with a smile on his face, that usually meant Mr. X wanted to hear some more from us, and we would have to come back tomorrow or the next week. If he came out with a frown, then it was on us, because we didn't do what we were supposed to do. Some companies wanted us, and Joe was happy, but nothing came of it because Joe always wanted what he called "front money," a phrase that at first meant nothing to us but essentially meant an advance payment against future recording royalties.

Finally, Barbara asked him, "What is front money?" He answered, "That's money that I get as your manager for bringing you to this company."

A bell went ding-dong in our collective heads. "Oh, this is the money that he gets." So, we inquired further, "Why do you get all the money? Why we can't get any of the money?" He explained that none of that money was for us. What did we know? We left it alone, but it kept burning in our ears. We didn't know how much he was asking for. Did he want tens, hundreds, or thousands of dollars, which in 1964 was a lot of money? Sometimes we could hear the conversations with the record company executives. Joe would ask for front money—and they would say, "What do you need front money for?" Joe's response involved a tearjerker story about the girls (meaning Barbara, Joan Marie, and me), who had family at home that they needed to support. He portrayed us as impoverished people, girls he picked up out of the gutter, that our parents didn't have a place to live, and we needed the money to send our parents so that they could buy food. None of this was true, and it was insulting. But Joe would spread that bullshit.

One day Joe and a record company man were having this discussion in front of us, and Barbara blurted out, "If you're giving out front money, then we need to get front money to send to our parents." The guy didn't blink. "I'll have my accountant write a check. Do you have an account in New York?" We said, no, we just had what we had at home in New Orleans. Joe began to steam because now we were talking to the people who were supposed to be giving Joe front money, but they switched and said they could give that money straight to us. One guy said they could get our parents' names and addresses and send them a certified cashier's check. This didn't hit Joe well, and when we left that one place, he was screaming and hollering; the gist of all the noise was that we were not supposed to say anything in these interviews.

After days of pounding the sidewalks, we finally ended up at the Brill Building.

Early in the twentieth century, an army of songwriters and music publishers could be found in lower Manhattan around West 28th Street between Fifth and Sixth Avenues. The area was known as Tin Pan Alley, and this is where you went to sell your tunes if you were a songwriter or to find songs if you were a performer. By the 1960s that core of the music industry shifted farther north to midtown Manhattan, to a group of buildings on Broadway, the most famous of which were 1650 Broadway and the Brill Building at 1619 Broadway. Inside these mid-rises were warrens of small offices where some of the best music in the country was being created. It's a little hard to visualize now how incredibly accessible, integrated, ingenuous, and even democratic the music industry was at the time the Meltones arrived in New York. The best description I ever read about the Brill Building was from writer Alan Betrock, and it went like this:

> There you could write a song or make the rounds of publishers until someone bought it. Then you could go to another floor and get a quick arrangement, lead sheet for $10, get some copies made at the duplication office, book an hour at a demo studio; hire some musicians and a singer that hung around; and finally cut a demo of the song. Then you could take it around the building to the record companies, publishers, artist's managers and even the artists themselves. If you made a deal, there were radio promoters to sell the record.

In the early 1960s, many of the more successful songwriters in the Brill Building or 1650 Broadway were young and part of a duo of lyricist and tunesmith. So you might find Burt Bacharach and Hal David, who wrote most of Dionne Warwick's great hits, or married couples such as Carole King and Gerry Goffin, who wrote "Will You Love Me Tomorrow" and many, many other hit records.

By the time we got to the Brill Building, we were a troop. We all arrived in an office where we met a pleasant couple with strong New York accents and what I finally figured out were the usual nervous, impatient movements of people who lived in Manhattan. Their names were Jeff Barry and Ellie Greenwich. While for Joe it was the same old spiel, I could see Jeff and Ellie eyeing us. Their faces lit up as if to say, "Where did you get these kids from?" The question for them was, can we sing? Of course, said Joe. Jeff sat down at the piano and we stood nearby. He played one note to bring us in, and we sang our "Thank You Mama." I could see they liked what they heard. Ellie asked if we had anything else, and we quickly organized a song, but I can't remember what it was.

In 1964 Ellie was twenty-four years old. She started writing songs as a teenager and sang demos all over town. Her first success came with a different writing partner, Tony Powers, and her first records to break the Top 40 were "Why Do Lovers Break Each Other's Hearts" by Bob B. Soxx and the Blue Jeans and "(Today I Met) The Boy I'm Gonna Marry" by Darlene Love. Then she met singer and songwriter Jeff Barry. They married in 1962 and soon were writing hit records (along with Phil Spector) for girl group singers. The year before we met Jeff and Ellie, they wrote such songs as "Then He Kissed Me" (#6 best seller) and "Da Doo Ron Ron" (#3 best seller) for the Crystals, and "Be My Baby" (#2 best seller) and "Baby, I Love You" (#24 best seller) for the Ronettes. The duo finished out 1963 with "Hanky Panky," sung by Tommy James & the Shondells, which went straight to the top of the charts. It was their first #1.

A few months later, the Meltones were in their office, and we were being suspiciously eyed. Jeff said to Ellie, "I bet they're going to tear that song up." Ellie nodded in agreement. I'm looking at Barbara and Joan Marie, thinking, What is he talking about? Jeff said, "Hold it, ladies, we're going to take a five-minute break." At that point Joe and everyone else left the room, as he had the Five Deejays to promote as well. It was just the three of us when Jeff and Ellie came back. Jeff went straight to the piano and sat down. Ellie stood close by. "Now, just listen to this. Even if you don't like it at first, we just want you to listen. We'll ask you about it afterward." Jeff played "Chapel of Love" on the piano. To us, the song had a slow, almost country beat. I was dubiously wondering, Is he going to want us to sing that? Ellie was watching us, and she could tell we weren't getting it. She stopped Jeff from playing it again. "Girls," she said, "you don't seem to like this song."

We rambled on in a disjointed response, yet still trying to be polite. We were all right with the wording but unsure enough about the melody that we asked, "Do we really have to sing it like that?" Ellie looked surprised. "Well, no," she said. "We were just trying to let you know how the melody goes. Can you do something else with it?"

Joan Marie and Barbara were two girls who would say what was on their minds. Joan Marie just blurted out, "Where did you get this song from?"

Ellie, very patient with us, said, "This is a song that Jeff and I wrote, and we think you girls can do something with it."

"Yeah, we probably could but not the way you want it," Joan Marie continued.

Ellie smiled. "We are going to leave you in here, and you do what you want to do with it, and we'll come back and listen."

"Sure." We knew enough to sound very, very positive. So, they said, "Go right ahead," and left us alone again in the room. I had a little bit of piano lessons, and I was able to find middle C on the piano. We sang the words in a softer version of what they presented to us, because neither Barbara, Joan Marie, nor I would have listened to that song on the radio the way it was first presented.

Going back to the original girl group singers that created and succeeded in the genre, the Chantels with "Maybe" (#15 best seller in 1958) and the Shirelles with "Will You Love Me Tomorrow" (#1 in 1960), "Soldier Boy" (#1 in 1962), and "Dedicated to the One I Love" (#3 in 1961), the sound format was lead and background. One singer would step forward and carry most of the song with the two or three other singers providing melody and fill. Jeff and Ellie's major girl group hits from 1963 such as "Be My Baby" and "Da Doo Ron Ron" were lead-and-background songs. Indeed, the top girl group songs from that year, including "He's So Fine" by the Chiffons, "My Boyfriend's Back" by the Angels, and "Heat Wave" by Martha & the Vandellas were all lead-and-background songs.

However, Barbara and I grew up singing with our mother in the church choir, where we sang in three-part harmony, our voices as one. We didn't do lead and background, because we never learned to sing that way. So the Meltones (soon to be the Dixie Cups) jumped the tracks. Our sound was three-part harmony, and that's how we treated "Chapel of Love" when left alone at the piano.

We might not have been so brave had we known that Jeff and Ellie were very successful songwriters. I'm not sure Joe even knew that. He introduced us and then left us with them. Jeff and Ellie at that point were just two more people we had to try to win over like everyone else Joe introduced us to in New York. They were blanks. We called them back into the room and sang "Chapel of Love" our way, in three-part harmony, and blew their heads off. They couldn't believe that in those five minutes, or however long it took us, we took that rough song and came out with that beautiful melody. They were so excited they called in two other guys, Jerry Leiber and Mike Stoller, to listen to us.

These were two new people we'd never heard of, but they were important. Leiber and Stoller, as they were generally referred to, had been a successful songwriting team since the early 1950s when they wrote a couple of songs, "Hound Dog" and "Jailhouse Rock," that helped make Elvis Presley a rock 'n' roller. In 1957 they would have eleven hit records on the chart, more than anyone else in the business. Their many, many hit records were written for a widely diverse group of performers: "Charlie Brown" for the Coasters, "There Goes My Baby" for the Drifters, "Lucky Lips" for Ruth Brown, "Stand by Me" for Ben E. King, "The Reverend Mr. Black" for the Kingston Trio, and "Is That All There Is?" for Peggy Lee. The two worked for Atlantic Records for many years, while also exploring their entrepreneurial side with independent labels such as Tiger and Daisy Records in 1960.

After listening to us, Mike Stoller said, "You know, we can start a new label with these girls from New Orleans." That's how Red Bird Records was born.

They wanted to put us on a new label because the Ronettes and Phil Spector didn't feel it was a good enough song to be released on the old label. They also had the Crystals record the song where Phil inserted Darlene Love's lead over LaLa Brooks's version, and then he shelved that recording as well. Nobody wanted to touch the song after that. It just didn't have what those people thought a hit record could be. We never met Phil Spector, although he is listed as one of the songwriters.

When Jerry and Mike came in, Jeff told them to just stand over there and listen. The two stood in a corner, because those rooms in the Brill Building were small. They folded their arms. Jeff played the song two or three times the way we were singing it, the way we had reoriented it. Little did we know we did the actual arrangement on "Chapel on Love." Jeff picked up what we were doing and replayed it on the piano. He had a tremendous ear. I was happy to hear him play, because I was always told in school that I had a wonderful ear for music, I could pick out the three notes in harmony with no problem. My music director at church would tell me, "You have a wonderful ear, you can hear the notes." Jeff could do the same.

Jerry and Mike looked at each other and told us to sing that again. Jeff played it with a smile wrapped around his head. Jerry asked, is that the "Chapel of Love" we had in the can, and Jeff nodded. Mike said, "We got to do something with it." That's when the four of them decided this is a new group, and they will make a new record company.

When they started talking about creating a new label, for all practical purposes the three of us could have been at the grocery store for how much attention they were paying to us. They were wildly talking this stuff, and none of it was hush-hush. At the time, we had no idea what all that excitement was about. We just wanted to sing.

At some point a photographer came. I have no idea who he was or when he came. We were upset because we didn't like this picture of us, although we were dressed for the moment. The photo is in black and white so you can't see we were wearing matching pink dresses and we had on no makeup. Not only was it a time when young ladies had to be dressed nicely when going out in public, but our parents taught us from childhood to be rightly attired. We got those dresses from the basement at Macy's department store. When we arrived in New York, we didn't have anything appropriate, only the outfits Barbara made for us when we appeared at the talent show, and that was too glitzy to walk around the streets of Manhattan and go visiting music executives. Sylvia might have recommended Macy's, because we certainly never heard of the store in New Orleans. Our parents had given us money for such a purpose. We got there soon after the store opened one morning, and we asked a saleslady about dresses. She looked at us and said, "You girls are so tiny, the best place to start looking would be in the basement. You might find something real cute." Later, we learned the basement was the bargain place in the store. It was in our price range; I don't think the dresses cost more than $15 apiece—and we fell in love with them. I think we added silver shoes with a moderate heel.

I could tell Ellie liked us, and sometime later she told a reporter, "Of all the young ladies I interviewed, we had the softest personality."

Often it's not just talent but timing that works in your favor—and that was the case with the Dixie Cups. Some performers struggle for years and years before catching the break of a lifetime, and some singers never get the break. In comparison, three girls from New Orleans, newly arrived in New York, walk into an office in the Brill Building and are handed what ends up to be a #1 song to be recorded on a spanking new label.

There is a backstory to all this that we didn't know at the time that had a lot to do with why our recording would inhale exalted air at first breath.

George Goldner, who had a great ear for pop music, started his first record company, Tico Records, in the late 1940s but really succeeded during the doo-wop era of the early 1950s. By that time he had created at least four record labels but, according to later press reports, had to sell his interest in these companies to pay off gambling debts. He started another label in 1957 called Roulette, sold his interest in that, and started Gone and End. The latter issued "Maybe" by the Chantels, the pioneering girl group recording act. Those labels were also sold as well. Well, one day Jerry and Mike were having lunch with Goldner and, since they were not having success with their own record companies, asked him to join up with them.

According to Ken Emerson, who wrote *Always Magic in the Air: The Bomp and Brilliance of the Brill Building Era*, this is what happened next:

> When Leiber mentioned some demos in his office, Goldner insisted on listening to them that very evening. "Are you going to stay there all night," (Leiber asked). He said, "I might." I (Leiber) gave him the keys and I came in at eleven o'clock the next morning and he was sitting behind my desk, not a hair out of place . . . He held up this acetate ("Chapel of Love") and said, "On my life. On my life . . ."
>
> He put it on, and I (Leiber) hated the fucking record.

All we saw was kindness that first day. Ellie and Jeff said to us, "Have you guys eaten anything?"

I said, "We ate some cereal this morning when we got up."

Ellie said, "We'll take you down to the Brill Building cafeteria."

To me, the food was fantastic and the atmosphere electric. Anyone who was recording at the time would stop by. That first day I remember meeting Chuck Berry. Ellie and Jeff brought us down, gave us the menus, and said, "Whatever you want, you can order it. Don't be afraid, we'll pick up the tab."

We were having a really good meal, when Joan Marie said, "Look, it's Johnny Mathis." He was and still is my favorite; I still have every album that he ever issued. I got so excited, I pulled at Barbara's sleeve. "Did you see who that was?" She whispered to me to calm down. So, I sat there like a little girl, but there was Johnny Mathis!

Afterward Joe showed up. Jeff and Ellie told Joe that Mike and Jerry were interested in the girls, and we would have to be at rehearsals at 10 a.m. Joe signed some papers. He wasn't much interested in the rehearsals, so he would drop us off at the Brill Building and go elsewhere. We wouldn't see him for a whole day.

CHAPTER FIVE

Chapel of Love

By our understanding, the Dixie Cups' rendition of "Chapel of Love" was to be on a new label because of the prior recordings of the song by the Ronettes and the Crystals and Phil Spector's complicated interest in those groups, the song, and even the companies involved in the recordings. At least that's what we were told.

The new label was called Red Bird Records, but the structure was a little complicated, because folded into it were Jerry and Mike's former labels Tiger and Daisy, and then the Blue Cat Records subsidiary was created to focus on more R&B-oriented records. Probably the biggest hit on the Blue Cat label was "The Boy from New York City" by the Ad Libs. The label also recorded an early Tiny Tim, the first go round for "Go Now" by Bessie Banks, and a fine record "Take Me for a Little While" by Evie Sands, which was recorded by many others.

Jerry purportedly didn't like "Chapel of Love" because it was so naively romantic. He had been in the business since rock 'n' roll was created and was desirous to create more serious or blues-oriented music, which he eventually would do. That was okay, because the success of Red Bird was to some extent based on the songwriting team of Jeff Barry and Ellie Greenwich, who could write those romantic ballads that teenage girls, who bought those 45s, really craved and bought by the millions. "Chapel of Love" was the first release by the Red Bird label, and it became the #1 best-selling record in the country, according to *Billboard*. Some months later another girl group, the Shangri-Las, boasted the company's second #1 song, "Leader of the Pack," written by George "Shadow" Morton along with Jeff and Ellie. Somewhere in between came songs by the Jelly Beans with "I Wanna Love Him So Bad" (#9 best seller), written by Jeff and Ellie, and the Shangri-Las' "Remember (Walking in the Sand)" (#5 best seller). George Morton wrote "Remember," but Jeff along with Artie Ripp produced it. Of the company's first thirty singles, eleven made it onto *Billboard*'s Top 40 listing. As Jerry once said, "Jeff and Ellie wrote most of it. They were the super-aces at making this type of material." This isn't to say Jerry—or Mike—neglected Barbara, Joan Marie, and me, but mostly we were left to work with Jeff and Ellie.

However, before anything was to happen for us, we had to ditch the Meltones name, as we were told it wasn't commercial. It was a bit too doo-woppish, and the world had moved on. Someone probably remembered there was a moderately successful group called the Quin-Tones that in 1958 had a similarly themed Top 20 hit record called "Down the Aisle of Love."

When I was informed that the Meltones was no longer workable as the name of a group, I asked why, and Ellie explained the music industry revolves around things the kids could relate to, and if we went out into the real world, Meltones was no longer "catchy." Jeff and Ellie at first suggested the very bizarre name Little Miss and the Muffets. We looked young, but we didn't look that young. The suggestion was met with a resounding "You got to be kidding." Please, we said, give us some time to come up with something better, and to their credit, Jeff and Ellie left it to us to devise another name. Joe wasn't with us, as he had made a trip to New Orleans to visit his real family. That was important, because at some point in the future he made the astounding claim that he owned the rights to the name. We had two things going on in our collective heads when forming the name. First was a possible reference to where we were from, the South. Second, as we started to look at girl group names, we saw a trend line to common things, such as, the Toys, the Chiffons, the Cookies, the Butterflys, the Jelly Beans. I don't know what the Shirelles referred to, but most other female groups seemed to reference items. What we came up with was the Dixie Cups.

Back in 1916 a single-use-paper-cup manufacturer began calling its product Dixie cups, and fifty years later, the ubiquitous name defined the item, the way the brand Kleenex once defined tissues. We thought the name with the word Dixie also defined us—we were southern girls. Since the name was also a corporate product, Jerry and Mike wrote to the Dixie company on our behalf, asking if we could use the name. Corporate executives were no fools. It would be like getting free advertising. Quickly, Dixie Cups wrote back, saying it was not a problem. We ended up incorporating the name for the singing group to protect ourselves from anyone trying to record or perform as us.

Joan Marie and I had never been in a recording studio before we came into Manhattan to record "Chapel of Love." Barbara had done studio work in New Orleans. Although this was all very exciting for us, we tried not to act like tourists visiting the Empire State Building. If I remember correctly, we were in the Mirasound Studios, where a number of other girl group records, such as "Da Doo Ron Ron" by the Crystals, had been recorded.

The experience was very comfortable, because back then you recorded with a live band, and in New Orleans we had sung with live musicians such as Arthur Neville's band. Everyone was there: Jeff and Ellie, Jerry and Mike, Joe Jones. Mike worked the boards. Jeff and Ellie were in the studio with us.

Mike and Jerry occasionally popped in and out of the control room. Mike would say something like, "I want to take it from . . .," or "Let's just try it once without the band, or without the drummer, or with just the bass player." No one at all made us feel that we didn't know what we were doing, and no one said, "OK, you all are not doing this right." There was no redo, redo, redo, and in the end that impressed Ellie, who said to us that none of the other girl groups were doing three-part harmony the way we did it. Ellie gave us no extra hints, because the Dixie Cups had worked out the arrangements at the Brill Building. It all went very quickly, including the recording of the B-side, "Ain't That Nice," an Earl King song we brought with us from New Orleans.

Ken Emerson wrote, "The New Orleans lilt in the rhythm section and Stoller's breezy horn arrangement added savor to the sentimentality, and Greenwich ran out of the control booth to augment the trio's wispy voices with a few extra 'yeah-yeahs.'" I don't remember Ellie doing that at all. Emerson, on the other hand, does get Mike's contribution in the "arrangements" for the song partly correct, and even that's important, because the record says the song was produced by Joe Jones. (The heavy lifting on the arrangements was done by Wardell Quezergue, who has gotten no credit for the song.)

With the recording studio crowded with veterans Jeff and Ellie and Jerry and Mike, you could be sure Joe had no voice in the recording of "Chapel of Love." At first I couldn't say if Jeff and Ellie or Jerry and Mike liked Joe. They just accepted his presence there in the studio. How he convinced everyone to give him production credits is a mystery.

The song's other credit that's a bit unusual is the songwriting team. It reads Jeff, Ellie, and Phil Spector. Jeff and Ellie we got to know well. Phil Spector we never met, never even saw him from a distance, but he was the ghost over so many of our recordings.

Lore has it that the first time Ellie met Phil, she cursed him out like a trucker with a flat tire, while the first time Jeff met him, they got along like a house afire. When Ellie met Jeff, they married, and professionally they brought Phil into their orbit. The first songs they all wrote together were hit records. "Then He Kissed Me" and "Da Doo Ron Ron" were both Top 5 records in 1963 for the Crystals. The trio also wrote the first two hit records for the Ronettes, including "Be My Baby," considered by *Billboard* magazine to be the best girl group song ever.

Phil liked to experiment with recording techniques and with his singers—to him all were interchangeable. Sometimes he would have both the Crystals and the Ronettes record the same song, which is what happened with "Chapel of Love." Fortunately for us, Phil disliked both recordings, and they were either never released or released and never promoted. When Ronnie Spector wrote her memoir, she recalled:

> The biggest reason for our slump was Phil, who had already started to lose interest in us as far back as April of 1964. That's when he recorded us doing "Chapel of Love" and then refused to release it as a single. We thought it was such a great record that we practically begged him to put it out. "No," he told us. "It doesn't sound like a hit. Forget about that one." Then The Dixie Cups' version came out and it was a smash! It was so depressing.

One would think that the appearance of "Chapel of Love" on the record charts would have pleased Phil, but it didn't. In a sense our success was a repudiation of his professional opinion that the song was no good. He never forgave us, and years later whenever our name came up for consideration for the Rock 'n' Roll Hall of Fame, he always blackballed us. According to Ken Emerson, the success of "Chapel of Love" created a rift between Jeff and Ellie and Phil. He didn't object to us recording the song but was embarrassed when it did so well because it "called into question his reputation as a producer and picker of hits."

Another ghost was George Goldner, whom we also never met. He was a partner with Jerry and Mike in forming Red Bird Records and would briefly end up with the label, so our success was great for him. Although a veteran of the recording industry, he left the production to Jerry and Mike and took over administration and promotion. We often heard George's name bandied about when we were at Red Bird, but if he wasn't helping us make records, we never really cared what he did. When we recorded "People Say," a big ad in the trades read: "Leiber-Stoller-Goldner present the Dixie Cups smash follow-up to 'Chapel of Love,' 'People Say.'"

We did the recording of "Chapel of Love" in the winter of 1964. It was cold in New York City, but hot in the studio. We sang it exactly as we had done in the Brill Building for Jeff and Ellie. The wonderful romantic lyrics:

Goin' to the chapel and we're gonna get ma-a-arried
Gee, I really love you
And we're gonna get ma-a-arried
Goin' to the "Chapel of Love"

The reason the tune worked so well as a Dixie Cups song was that we eschewed the lead and background. I believe we were the only girl group at the time working in three-part harmony. It was a very different sound. After we finished, Jerry and Mike told us we could go home, that the rest was up to them to get it released. They did whatever they had to do as producers and promoters, really believing in the song.

After that first recording session, the Dixie Cups flew home to New Orleans, which was also an interesting point, because Joe always fostered the notion that he picked us up out of the gutter, put us in a car, and drove us to New York, and when the recording session was over, he put us on a Greyhound bus to go back to where we came from. Joe's song and dance about discovering the Dixie Cups always got under my skin, because our mother always worked, while it was Joe and his warehouseman father who had to come up from poverty. The Hawkins family had already arrived.

We left New York and returned to New Orleans, a city that seemed quiet in comparison. We needed to decompress, take it easy, visit with our mom, and try not to dwell too much on all that we had accomplished, that is, making a record, which still at that point didn't mean all that much to me. I could hope for a radio station to play our song, but that seemed more a dream than reality.

We went back to our old lives, doing the things we used to do. And then!

I was in the living room, doing my chores and listening to the radio. I heard our song, and like a congregant listening to the church choir, I started automatically singing with the song until I realized, "That's our song!" I went flying up the stairs, calling my mom. Alarmed, she said, "What, what is the matter?" as if something was wrong. I screamed, "It's our song, it's on the air, it's on the radio!" Realizing there was no catastrophe, she said, extremely blasé, "Calm down, it will be on the air a lot of times." But I didn't understand that. I yelled for Barbara, who was upstairs in her room. We listened. The local deejay said, "This is New Orleans's own Dixie Cups," and, "They are Mrs. Hawkins's daughters," because my mom wrote a column, like Ann Landers, in the local newspaper, where she would give advice to teenagers. The New Orleans disc jockey played that up, Mrs. Hawkins's girls have a new record. That all began on a Saturday. Jeff called sometime during that coming week. He asked me if my mom was home. I answered affirmatively. He asked if there was another line she could pick up on, and I said yes. My mom picked up the upstairs phone, and Barbara and I were downstairs jammed together at the telephone receiver. Jeff said, "I'm sure we have a hit with this record, and we are going to be sending for the girls in a few weeks, but before that we need to get things arranged." My mother asked, "What are you talking about?" He said we needed a decent place to live and get ready for promotions and appearances.

Phyllis, the receptionist at Red Bird, called and told us, "We are getting everything together, and then we'll mail the information to you." That took some time, and when everything was arranged, she sent along a travel package. My mother asked about the weather in New York. She was concerned about me because, with me being so skinny, with no meat on my bones, I tended to get cold quickly. It was still winter in the Northeast, so my mom cautioned, "Rosa Lee, get your mind set, because you don't like the cold weather. But you dropped out of college to pursue this career, so you have to do what you have to do to make it." Like a petulant child, I answered, "If I get too cold, I'm coming home."

When we got back to New York, we stayed at the Bryant Hotel in Manhattan. We were given a suite, which wasn't as great as it sounds—it had three beds and a kitchenette.

One of the first things that needed to be done was promotional pictures.

When we first met with Jeff and Ellie and sang "Chapel of Love" for them, a photographer came into the small room and asked us to gather around for a picture. So Ellie sat at the piano, Jeff behind, and the Dixie Cups crowded in. That day was all a swirl of events, and we weren't quite ready for our moment. Among the three of us, there is only one smile. Although this is probably the earliest photo of the Dixie Cups, we were upset when we saw the result; we just didn't like this photo. Only Ellie looked like she knew what she was doing.

Now with "Chapel of Love" rising on the charts, we needed professional pictures, and Jeff and Ellie brought in Maurice Seymour—actually two brothers, Maurice and Seymour Zeldman, who had been taking pictures of artists and entertainers since 1929. Singers Tony Bennett, Harry Belafonte, and Della Reese sat for Maurice. Now it was the Dixie Cups' turn. It wasn't as easy as you would think. First, we had to have outfits. Phyllis took us to a department store for matching dresses. Then we had to have our hair done. Finally, someone came in and showed us how to apply makeup, because none of us wore it at that time. Up until that moment, my mother had allowed me to use only a small amount of lip gloss with color, and a bit of mascara.

After the photos came our first appearances, at sock hops (teenage girls would take off their shoes to dance in their stocking feet), with radio deejays and local television shows. I can barely recall our first presentation. It was at a high school gym. There was a band on stage. It was really crowded, and the kids, all of them white, were jammed up against that stage, so when the deejay introduced us and we walked out, three Black girls, a brief hush settled over the entire room. No one knew the Dixie Cups were Black, or, in the 1960s vernacular, no one knew the Dixie Cups were Negro. We did a lot of quick radio interviews, which mentioned only that we were from the South, and people in the North had little concept of southern Blacks beyond stereotypes. Barbara, Joan Marie, and I always spoke carefully, in grammatically correct complete sentences with no slang, so young northern teenagers who listened to these interviews assumed we were white. We did these sock hops for two years before we came to one that was integrated.

Sometimes at these sock hops there would be two or three groups. It was all so rushed we never knew more than we had to. Who were the other performers? It was anyone trying to make it at the time, including on one occasion the Rolling Stones. We worked with all the big disc jockeys on the East Coast, especially those in New York, such as Murray the K and Cousin Brucie.

We also had to learn the business. At first Jerry and Mike simply told us how successful the record was and how big it was going to be. The ecstatic Ellie said to us, "We got a hit, ladies, we got a hit." So, we started picking up the industry magazines, *Billboard*, *Cashbox*, and *Record World*, to see how we were doing. When we opened up to the all-important Top 100 record charts, Ellie instructed us on finding our song, how to track it, what it was the week before, even what the iconic "bullet" meant. We were like first-graders at an elementary school.

We came back to New York. The Bryant was only temporary until Red Bird and Joe Jones found us a permanent place to live. There were two structures, the Westerly and the 888 Building, that catered to entertainers, musicians, even go-go girls (dancers at the local music clubs). We chose the Westerly and just slipped right into our surroundings. This time when we came to New York, it was for five years.

All wasn't bright lights and stardom for us. Once you make the record charts, you have to work hard to stay there. And like everyone else, you have to earn money to live. Joe was our manager, and we misguidedly left our financial arrangements in his hands. We thought we worked for Joe Jones, and he had the upper hand because when things got bad between one of the Dixie Cups and Joe, he would threaten to throw that person out of the group. The true situation was that he worked for the Dixie Cups, and at first we were too young and untrained to realize it.

To some extent Joe worked his game on Jerry and Mike as well. Since he had an automobile, he took charge of our promotions, brought us around to the different disc jockeys, radio stations, and dances in the Northeast. This wasn't out of benevolence or even due to his driving skill. Joe knew where he could make money between the cracks in the system. For example, when we would visit radio stations, it was always at night, and it was not just a free appearance; Joe would expect a payoff for bringing the Dixie Cups in for a deejay interview. For the special events like a dance, he would pay himself as our manager, director of promotions, and driver. The Dixie Cups even paid for the gas in his car. All this he would have written down and neatly tabulated to show us in case we asked. So, let's say the Dixie Cups would be paid $1,500 to sing at a dance or teenage sock hop. By the time Joe finished adjusting the debits on his ledger, there might be fifteen dollars left for Barbara, Joan Marie, and me. Barbara would lament, "We didn't drop out of college for this." That five dollars for each of us, even back in the mid-1960s, didn't buy you much of a dinner.

When "Chapel of Love" sold its first three million records, we were told we would be getting our first royalty check. We were so excited, thinking we would finally be getting some big money, thousands of dollars, since we knew how well the record had done. We rattled off all the things we were going to buy and things we were going to do: get new furniture for the apartment, send money to our moms, or just go on a big shopping spree. Then we opened our envelopes. Stunned, we had to sit down. Each of us got a check for $482.67. A printout showed how expenses, fees, and advances decimated our earnings, but Red Bird Records—and Joe Jones, stealing through advances—did all right.

I always claim Joe Jones had it so easy with the Dixie Cups that he never made a serious attempt to expand his roster of clients. After "Chapel of Love" came out, other singers did contact Joe. There was one white group that sent Joe a dub, a copy of a record they wanted to record, and wanted to have Joe manage them. Joe didn't answer the inquiry. We said, "Aren't you going to even get back to them?" He shook his head. "Nah, that's a bunch of white boys, I'm not interested." The group eventually had hit records and became famous. Joe would also sign very pretty young girls he wanted to sleep with. That never worked out well for him.

Joe had loyalty—not to the Dixie Cups—but to other male singers he knew from New Orleans. That loyalty, however, had economic limits. Back in 2000, the Neville Brothers published a memoir, and I learned something I never knew before.

In the early 1960s, Charles Neville had been in jail on a narcotics charge, and when he was released, he hooked up with Joe Jones, who was setting him up in New York at our expense. Apparently, Charles didn't know Joe, but Arthur and Aaron did, and they put him together with Joe, who signed papers saying Charles would road-manage the Dixie Cups. That allowed Charles to be paroled in New York City. Charles wrote, "For a week or so, I helped out The Dixie Cups. But that was just a temporary job set up by Joe Jones to legitimize my parole." Charles moved into the Bryant Hotel at Fifty-Fourth Street and Broadway. He earned from his new job enough money "for one week's rent." We never knew all that. Charles never went on the road with us as manager, horn player, or anything. I remember Charles got out of jail and came to New York. I knew he was staying at the Bryant, because he came with Joe to visit us at our apartment. That was it. We didn't see him again in New York and had no idea Joe was doing someone a good turn—with money that was not coming out of his pocket.

Also coming to New York was Aaron Neville, who arrived after the success of "Tell It Like It Is." He stayed with us at our apartment for a short period of time, as Joe was going to take on the management of his career. Joe got Aaron a few gigs to start. Frank Sinatra heard Aaron sing and contacted Joe. Frank thought his management company could do a better job handling Aaron, but he would be generous. He assured Joe he didn't want to steal his talent away from him, that Joe would still be Aaron's manager on paper while Frank's company would take over the business end of Aaron's career. Joe asked for front money. Frank's people asked, "For what?" Joe gave them the old sob sorry, that Aaron was married and his wife was in New Orleans with children. Frank's people said fine, they would send a check to Aaron. Frank went so far as to make an appointment for Aaron to get some suits and shoes, then come in and record. Since Joe could not get the front money to come to him directly, he blew off Frank Sinatra. Aaron ended up staying with Joe until he got tired of him, and then he left.

Such was also the case with Alvin Robinson, a well-known session musician in New Orleans who had played in Joe Jones's band back home. Joe got him signed to Jerry and Mike's Tiger label, where he recorded a song, "Something You Got," written by another New Orleans musician, Chris Kenner. Joe had himself listed as the arranger. Kenner had written such wonderfully danceable tunes as "I Like It Like That" and "Land of 1,000 Dances," but "Something You Got" was a deep "soul" song. It did reasonably well. The June 27, 1964, *Cashbox* record chart listed "Something You Got" at #67, with a red star indicating it was ascending. Then the momentum stalled, and it ended up rising only to #52 on the record charts. Jerry preferred the blues songs and moved Robinson to Red Bird Records, where he recorded the Jerry and Artie Butler song "Down Home Girl," with Joe once again taking arranger credits. Jerry declared it the best record to be recorded on the Red Bird label, but it was a commercial failure.

Alvin Robinson was our guitar player when we had to go on a gig and bring a musician along. He was a nice guy, soulful with a great voice. He was also a perfect patsy for Joe, who took advantage of him. At first Red Bird wouldn't give Joe front money for Alvin, although he kept trying. Joe would go to Jerry and Mike and whine that Alvin had a wife and child back home and needed money. Joe would go through a similar scheme involving the Dixie Cups, saying how we were impoverished and how Barbara and I needed to support our ailing mother. We didn't know Joe had continued to misuse our real story, and neither did Alvin. Whatever front money Joe got, he kept.

I don't know if Alvin ever found out Joe had squeezed him, and we didn't find out until we finally got our diminutive royalty check for "Chapel of Love" and saw in the big printout, "advance," "advance," "advance," and each entry had a date and amount. So we went to the bookkeeper, whose name was Florence, to complain, because we had never come up to her office to ask for money—ever. Our mother had a good job in New Orleans and did not need our help. Florence said to us, "Your manager was always coming up here saying you needed money to send to parents for rent or for this or that." When she saw tears streaming down my cheeks, Florence said, "I'm really sorry." Too late. The damage was done to us.

The other problem Alvin faced was that Joe wasn't getting him any bookings. In this girl group era, and with only a moderate hit, he wasn't as easy a sell, and Joe never tried that hard. Basically, he kept Alvin dangling on a string.

"Down Home Girl" was somewhat of a comic song that was soon covered by the Rolling Stones and then others. The opening lyrics went like this:

Well I swear your perfume baby
Is made out of turnip greens
Every time I kiss you girl
It tastes like pork and beans

Unlike with the Dixie Cups, Jerry really was keen on Alvin's R&B-infused sound, so he and Mike wrote "Bottom of My Soul" for him. Maybe they were just a year or two ahead of their time, because that song too disappeared without a trace.

That was certainly not the case with "Chapel of Love," which goes on and on and on.

The song benefited from perfect timing. It was released around the beginning of spring 1964, and spring is always for lovers and those to be wed. The record turned out to be a monster. By mid-June it was the #1 record in the country and stayed there for three weeks. It also hung onto the Top 100 record charts for eleven weeks total.

The year 1964 was, of course, the year the Beatles arrived in America and conquered all. On February 1, "I Want to Hold Your Hand" landed as the #1 song in the country, and through "She Loves You" and "Can't Buy Me Love," the Beatles kept that #1 position until May 9, when Louis Armstrong's "Hello, Dolly!" took it, followed for two weeks by Mary Wells with Motown's first #1 record, "My Guy." The Beatles flooded the charts in 1964 with almost twenty Top 40 records, and on May 30 they were back in the #1 position with "Love Me Do." Then the Dixie Cups arrived, and "Love Me Do" was done at #1.

According to *Cashbox*, on June 6, 1964, "Chapel of Love" was the #1 record, followed by "Love Me Do," "My Guy," "Love Me with All Your Heart" by Ray Charles, and "Hello, Dolly!" On June 13 "Chapel of Love" was still #1, but in the #2 slot with a star was "A World without Love" by Peter and Gordon, followed by "Love Me with All Your Heart," "Love Me Do," and "My Guy." The next chart was June 27, and "A World without Love" was now #1, followed by "I Get Around" by the Beach Boys, "Chapel of Love" (after three weeks at #1 on *Cashbox*), "My Boy Lollipop" by Millie Small, and with a star at #5 "People" by Barbra Streisand. A lot of good songs, a lot of good singers, and a lot of competition. Still, a month later "Chapel of Love" remained on the charts.

From 1958 through 1965, it seemed as if a hundred or more songs by all-female groups twirled into the radio stations. Only a few have stood the test of time. "Chapel of Love" is one that has over the years become more, not less, esteemed. Not only has it been used in at least twenty-five movies (*Legend, Arthur, Full Metal Jacket, Father of the Bride*, among them) and television shows (*GLOW, Welcome to Marwen, Glee*, etc.), but writers continue to rank it as one of the best. Dave Marsh, in his book *The Heart of Rock & Soul: The 1001 Greatest Singles Ever Made*, ranks it #276. He wrote, "Finger snaps, light horn riffs, snazzy uptown shuffle from the drums, a touch of vibes, singing more unison than harmony.... Record still makes the case for giving it up and getting hitched seem damned persuasive."

Rolling Stone magazine's list of the 500 Greatest Songs of All Time checks "Chapel of Love" in at #284. The magazine noted, "Spector took two cracks at recording 'Chapel,' but the Ronettes and Crystals left him flat. Leiber and Stoller took it to the novice Dixie Cups; the hopeful harmonies were just what the nuptial ditty called for."

CHAPTER SIX

People Say

Along with our first singles released to the record-buying public, we also recorded an album, which hit the market in August 1964, less than six months after we entered the recording studio for the first time.

The album was also called *Chapel of Love*, and when we initially saw it, we were very disappointed, because it didn't have our picture anywhere on the album jacket. These were still segregated times in the country, and Red Bird Records, like other music publishers, tried to hide the fact that certain popular singers were Black, out of fear some teenagers wouldn't buy the records, especially in the South. Take a look at the Shirelles' first album, *Tonight's the Night*, from 1961. The cover is a meaningless mélange of items, from a prom dress, to flowers, to a table with a picture of a white boy. The *Chapel of Love* album was no less silly and obscure. It shows what looks to be the top of a wedding cake with small statues of a groom and bride—looking very white—along with discarded Dixie Cups.

Red Bird's ability to produce an album so quickly was due to having us in the studio whenever we weren't on the road, and having a ready supply of songs for us to record. The album boasted ten songs. One, "Iko Iko," was written by the Dixie Cups, and I talk it about in another chapter. Three of the songs were written by our friend from New Orleans, Earl King under different names:

"Thank You Mama, Thank You Papa," by Ernestine Gaines, "Ain't That Nice" by Earl King Johnson, and "I'm Gonna Get You Yet" by Earl King Johnson.

Earl stood taller than me. He was a real gentleman, treating us as young ladies instead of just teenagers, although he would sometimes refer to us as "the little girls" when he was peevish or when he slipped into music business lingo, and we had no idea what he was talking about. Earl would often stand around as we practiced his songs, and he would always compliment us on the way we sang. He was very patient, realizing we were new to the recording studio. He liked my voice because it was deeper than Barbara's and Joan Marie's and he wanted me to get my sound out more instead of just being in the background.

As I mentioned, Earl King sometimes used a pseudonym, but alterations of names often had to do with a scheme by Joe to negate Earl's (and other's) authorship of songs. The other six songs were either written by Jeff and Ellie or Jeff, Ellie, and Phil Spector. It wasn't as if Jeff and Ellie were writing a slew of songs at the moment for us. Many of these, especially the ones cowritten by Phil Spector, had been written for other performers but never released. These were "in the can" as we used to say in the business. "Chapel of Love" was a good example.

Another case in point is the second song on the album, "Gee the Moon Is Shining Bright," written by Jeff, Ellie, and Phil Spector. The original title was "Why Don't They Let Us Fall in Love," and it was written for the Ronettes, but according to legend Phil didn't think it was a good enough record and issued "Be My Baby" with its Wall of Sound instead. Good choice, as "Be My Baby" has become an American classic. But that didn't mean "Why Don't They Let Us Fall in Love" was a bad record. Early in 1964 Phil allowed the record to be released as a Ronnie Spector song but attributed it to Veronica. It did not chart. So it came to the Dixie Cups at a recording session, and we recorded it under a completely different name. The new title was lifted from one of the lines in the song. Red Bird slowly released as singles four songs from the "Chapel of Love" album, and "Gee the Moon Is Shining Bright" wasn't let go until 1965—bad timing for a number of reasons—and it never even cracked Billboard's Top 100 records. Someone, however, did take notice of the song. When Sonny & Cher a year later put together their first album, *Look at Us*, with their monster hit "I Got You Babe" on it, one of the other songs on the album was "Why Don't They Let Us Fall in Love," with a very affecting lead by Cher.

To see how record company executives rechanneled old songs to which they owned the rights, here are the lyrics to both versions of the same song ("Why Don't They Let Us Fall in Love" by Spector-Greenwich-Barry; "Gee the Moon Is Shining Bright" by Greenwich-Barry-Spector):

First, the interior lyrics to the Dixie Cups' "Gee the Moon Is Shining Bright":

Gee the moon is shining bright
I can't wait to hold you tight
Gee the moon is shining bright
I can't wait to hold you tight

Now, the similar lyrics to "Why Don't They Let Us Fall in Love":

Gee, the moon is shining bright
Wish I could go out tonight
Why don't they let us fall in love?
Why don't they let us fall in love?

Back in 1963 Jeff and Ellie formed their own pop group, the Raindrops, and had moderate success with "What a Guy" (*Billboard* #41 in 1963) and "The Kind of Boy You Can't Forget" (*Billboard* #17 in 1963). In 1964 a Raindrops album dropped on the market. One of the songs on the album was Jeff and Ellie's "Another Boy Like Mine." Jeff and Ellie never liked to waste a song, so it also appeared on the *Chapel of Love* album. In a later session, we recorded "Little Bell," which, when Ellie and Jeff introduced it to us, we liked immediately. It was another lush, romantic song. Red Bird finally decided to release it toward the end of 1964. In Jeff and Ellie's waste-not, want-not way of doing business, "Another Boy Like Mine" was tacked on as the B-side to "Little Bell." Poor "Little Bell" suffered from lack of promotion, because the radio stations had to deal with a number of very good Dixie Cups releases around the same time, including "You Should Have Seen the Way He Looked at Me" and, a little later, "Iko Iko." This sweet little song, "Little Bell," got lost, ending up just outside Top 40, at *Billboard* #51.

Two other Ellie, Jeff, and Phil Spector songs on the album had been tried out with Phil Spector's favorite groups but basically ended up gathering dust on Red Bird shelves, and since no song should be wasted, the two were passed to the Dixie Cups. These were "All Grown Up," which was released by the Crystals in July 1964, a month before our album, but went nowhere, probably because it wasn't promoted. This one didn't even make the B-side of any of our records. The other was "Girls Can Tell," which was recorded by the Crystals and the Ronettes. This one ended up as the B-side to "People Say."

"People Say" was our second release and our second-best-selling record. It was released in July 1964, and by mid-August it charted as the #12 best-selling song in the country, according to *Billboard*. Ellie and Jeff wrote it without Phil Spector.

The recording went smoothly. Basically, what was happening is that Ellie and Jeff had these songs in the can, and after we would finish with one song, if it wasn't too late in the evening, we recorded another. Then we would come back the next week, and Ellie and Jeff would introduce another song. They always would play the song as it was written—we never asked who wrote it, although after a while we figured it out that it was mostly Ellie and Jeff. They would ask us, "How do you like this?" Ellie understood us and would always give us a moment with the next song. She would say, "OK, you don't like this. You all go on and do what you want to do to it," which we did. We were so willing to work with Ellie and Jeff that Ellie fell in love with us, which she proclaimed on more than one interview. "My Dixie Cups, they were so easy to work with," Ellie told one writer. "If they were given a song that they didn't like, they would say, 'Do you really want us to do it like that?' Then they would rework it."

We completely redid the harmony on "People Say," because the way Ellie and Jeff played it, the song was just lead and background. We told Ellie, "We don't sing that way," and Ellie asked, "How would you do it?" We sang it the way we would do it with the three-part harmony. Little did we know, we again were actually doing arrangements. Ellie and Jeff just gave us the opportunity to record it as we saw fit, although we didn't know anything about making records. Jerry and Mike produced. When they said sing, we sang.

If I remember correctly, we had been on a tour, and in between dates Jeff and Ellie presented us with "People Say." When we had gotten back to New York, Joe said we have another session, and we started rehearsing "People Say" immediately. Everyone liked the results, and just as with "Chapel of Love," Red Bird Records went all out for us, with advertisements in publications like *Billboard* proclaiming "The Dixie Cups' Next Hit Record."

On June 13, 1964, the record made the *Cashbox* charts, entering at Number 70, sandwiched between "Walk Don't Run '64" by the Ventures and "How Do You Do It" by Gerry & the Pacemakers. There were no highlights or bullets for any of these records. "People Say" had a slow climb as indicated by the record charts. On July 18, 1964, *Cashbox* put all three records in its "Sure Shots" box along with "Ain't She Sweet" by the Beatles, but the real indicator of our song picking up speed was *Cashbox*'s "Radio Active" chart for July 1964, which had "People Say" as #1 with 75 percent of radio stations adding the song to programs scheduled. We were just ahead of "Tell Me" by the Rolling Stones, which was the British group's first hit in the United States. At the beginning of August, "People Say" topped out at #12 on the *Billboard* record charts. What was #1 at the time? "A Hard Day's Night" by the Beatles. Still, it was a good showing for us, and "People Say" became our second gold record in a seven-month period. I don't know if any other girl group has done that, except, perhaps, the Supremes.

The local newspapers were proud of us. On December 31, 1964, one New Orleans newspaper showed a nice picture of us with the headline: "Two Gold Records in 7 Months." The caption read:

> Pictured above are New Orleans' own Dixie Cups, who, although they have only been recording for about 7 months, have two gold records: "Chapel of Love" and "People Say." . . . Inset, Mrs. Lucille Hawkins, mother of Rosa Lee and Barbara. Mr. & Mrs. William Johnson are the parents of Joan. The group is managed by Joe "You Talk Too Much" Jones, also of New Orleans. All music lovers should be anxious to purchase The Dixie Cups' recently released album, *Chapel of Love*, which includes both gold records.

Another New Orleans paper ran a different picture of us, with the headline: "Personalities of the Week." This caption read "The trio of N.O. lovelies are on a worldwide tour and playing to SRO crowds. The Dixie Cups joined the ranks of big time stars when they received their two Gold Records for 'Chapel of Love' and 'People Say.'"

This record also has gained its fans over the years, and *Billboard* included it as #53 on its list of 100 Greatest Girl Group Songs of All-Time ("Chapel of Love" at #33).

Billboard wrote:

> Those damn sideline haters, always providing their unsolicited sniping as to why girl group romances won't last—The Dixie Cups don't wanna hear it, and on "People Say," they shake'em off in exhilarating fashion over a snapping beat, declaring "I don't really care what 'People Say.'" Despite these assertions, the group's own intro gives away their lingering insecurity: "Don't you ever hurt me, if you do/Everything they're saying will be true."

As mentioned, the B-side was "Girls Can Tell." When a song was presented to us, we were always honest with Ellie and Jeff and said if we did or didn't like the material. Songs, such as "Girls Can Tell," that had a history were presented to us as if they had just seen the light of day for the very first time. No one said, for example, we tried it with the Crystals and it didn't work, and now we are going to try it with you—nobody said that to us. As for "Girls Can Tell," to this day, I have not heard a version of the song by the Crystals, although they were supposed to have recorded it first.

We had the right voices for these songs that had been in the can forever. When Ellie and Jeff decided to pull a record, from that point on, the music was written around what we did as singers. We didn't do what the music said; the music did what we said. "Girls Can Tell" was just another song they brought out of the back room. Ellie played it for us on the piano. She said, "Let's take a lunch break and play along with it when we come back." The whole time we were sitting there in the cafeteria of the Brill Building, the melody was stuck in our collective mind. Throughout the lunch we were humming the melody. By the time we went back upstairs, Ellie asked, "Are you ready?" In our heads we played around with the melody, just having fun with it. The official arrangement was by Mike Stoller.

There was also an unofficial arranger to all our songs, including "Chapel of Love," and that was Wardell Quezergue. Joe had known him from New Orleans, probably going back to his days when he got out of the service. He was already a well-known arranger and producer by the 1960s. Basically, all of the songs on our first album that were written by Earl King were arranged by Wardell, although Joe managed to share credit on each. Wardell was so good, he could just listen to us sing and then go ahead and start writing the music for the song. Wardell was also a real sweetheart of a guy, often saying to us, "I do this because I love it, I don't do it for the money," an attitude that only meant Joe was constantly taking advantage of him. Wardell never made any money working with Joe, but his time would come soon afterward. In 1965 he arranged and produced Robert Parker's "Barefootin'," which became a Top 10 record. Robert was another New Orleans singer. The Crescent City tentacles were strong even in New York.

In a sign of things to come, Joe was having fits in the control room, because no one would let him do anything, touch anything. However, we were still using his band, because it was a damn good band. Ellie and Jeff might add another trumpet or sax player, but Joe's basic group of musicians, all New Orleans veterans, were in the studio with us. For example, Smokey Johnson was our drummer. He was so good that when we went out to California to do the *Shindig!* show and we walked into the studio, Billy Preston, the show's keyboard player, greeted us warmly. After introductions he said, "Come over here for a second, I have a question for you. How many drummers did you use for 'Two-Way-Poc-Away' and some of the other songs that you guys have on your album?" "Er," I said, "What do you mean how many drummers?" He repeated the question, so we answered the obvious, "Just one, Smokey Johnson." He said, "No way. Do you know how long it took me to dissect what he was doing? It took me all day." Smokey had been in the military and saw action. Part of his foot was amputated, and as a result they put a screw in it. When Smokey would get hot, that foot would, pardon the metaphor, run away from him. Whoever is listening closely to our songs thinks, Damn, there's another drummer in there. That's how good Smokey was.

We were so inexperienced. We recorded our first two songs, "Chapel of Love" and "People Say," and we had big hits. We thought that was the norm, but it was an anomaly. We eventually learned there were so many girl groups that had been singing for five or six years and were still trying to get that first hit. When we recorded "Chapel of Love" and "People Say," Mike would tell us, "That's a wrap," and weeks later the songs were released and became hits. We didn't have the opportunity for humiliation—but that time would come much more quickly than we ever expected.

There was so much going on with Joe and Jerry and Mike that Red Bird had stopped pushing us. With our first couple of songs, every time you opened a *Billboard* or *Cashbox* magazine you saw our faces. Red Bird was pushing us with every trick George Goldner had up his sleeve. Many nice stories were written about us. By the time of "Little Bell," there wasn't much push anymore. This was for two reasons. By that point everyone at Red Bird was tired of Joe. They didn't trust him, and they certainly didn't like the way he was treating the Dixie Cups.

Secondly, the world of music was changing rapidly, and the old order was breaking up. One might say divorce was in the air, and I employ the term every which-way you might think of.

I used the word "inexperienced" to describe our first months in the big-time musical world, and the word is useful to depict our personal relations with those at Red Bird Records who were closest to us, that is, Ellie and Jeff. Every time we would go to Red Bird to record or be introduced to a new tune, Ellie and Jeff were the ones who worked with us. They were a handsome couple, very professional and dedicated to the music they were making. They were the perfect couple for the Dixie Cups, but they just weren't the perfect couple for each other. We had no clue that the marriage of Ellie and Jeff was on the rocks. They never discussed their issues in front of us. They didn't have personal arguments when we were around, and no one associated with Red Bird ever mentioned problems between the two. This ignorance was a two-way street. As Ellie later told an interviewer, "Literally, they [the artists] were vehicles for the songs. So we knew them as far as rehearsing them, but knowing them? No."

To the Dixie Cups, they were always Ellie and Jeff. The songs of Ellie and Jeff or Ellie and Jeff and Phil Spector that we recorded were always deeply romantic and about marriage or boyfriends. I suppose we assumed that if Ellie and Jeff were writing about romance, it was something they felt between them. So, if they no longer had that same relationship, perhaps it got harder to crank out those kinds of songs. If that was going on, we didn't know about it. What did happen was that the pressure to be in the studio to record new material began to ease as 1964 turned into 1965.

One more recording from earlier in 1964 charted in November of that year. "You Should Have Seen the Way He Looked at Me," which was a Top 40 hit, topped out at #39. This was another Ellie and Jeff record, produced by Jerry and Mike. The arrangement was by Artie Butler. The B-side was "No True Love," which was not an Ellie and Jeff song, so Joe was able to get his name on the record as arranger.

For the Dixie Cups, as 1965 rolled around, such fine songs as "You Should Have Seen the Way He Looked at Me," stopped coming around. Ellie and Jeff were experimenting with independence, doing recordings under their own names. By October they were separated and before the year ended signed divorce papers.

Meanwhile, after more than a decade in the rock 'n' roll business, Jerry and Mike were becoming burnout cases and itching to go do something else. In April 1966 they sold their interest in Red Bird to partner George Goldner. The underside, or other side, of this story is that George Goldner was reportedly an inveterate gambler and ran up a heap of personal debts to mob-controlled interests, which made Jerry and Mike nervous enough to leave the company. The label finally collapsed in 1968, by which time all the rainmakers (the Dixie Cups, the Shangri-Las, and the Ad-Libs) from Red Bird's and Blue Cat's glory days of 1964 to 1965 were long gone.

The divorces of Ellie and Jeff and Red Bird Records and Jerry and Mike all were preceded by the divorce of the Dixie Cups from Red Bird Records early in 1965. This separation had nothing to do with the Dixie Cups; it was all about Joe squabbling with Jerry and Mike.

"Iko Iko" was finally released in the United States in the spring of 1965, and it looked like it was going to be a hit record. Joe was in New Orleans during the recording, and his name was not listed in the formal paperwork as writer, arranger, or producer—nothing. Joan, Barbara, and I were listed as the writers. Joe tried and tried to get Mike and Jerry to change the paperwork so he could be listed as a writer, although he had nothing to do with the record, but they knew a scam when they saw it and said no. Then Joe just reverted to his Joe side. He was going to show Mike and Jerry and Red Bird what he could do about that situation. What he did was go to ABC-Paramount Records and let them know the Dixie Cups were available.

American Broadcasting-Paramount Theatres formed a records division in 1955, moving quickly into rock 'n' roll and scoring in the late 1950s with Paul Anka's "Diana," Danny & The Juniors' "At the Hop," and the Elegants' "Little Star," among other hits. By the 1960s the label jumped aggressively into R&B, signing Ray Charles away from Atlantic, and in 1961 adding the Impressions, among others. Also in 1961 the label was renamed ABC-Paramount Records. It never had a strong female talent roster, although Edie Gormé was the first act it signed as a new record label. ABC-Paramount did release in 1958 the pre–girl group record "Born Too Late" by the Poni-Tails, and it recorded early Maxine Brown and Baby Washington records, but mostly missed the girl group era, so when Joe Jones showed up at ABC-Paramount's front door, they let him in.

We had no idea there was trouble with Red Bird. Whatever was going on with Joe and the label was kept from the Dixie Cups. One day Joe said to us we would no longer be singing with Mike and Jerry and that we were going to ABC. When we asked why, he said, "That's what happens in this business"—as if that explained anything. As we were to learn, Joe received a lot of "upfront" money for bringing us to ABC. We girls didn't get a dime.

The next thing we knew, we were at ABC-Paramount, and the record people there were loving our sound, our three-part harmony, saying that we were going to be the next—I don't know—the next Andrews Sisters, McGuire Sisters, whatever sisters. We were rushed into the studio to record some singles and an album called *Riding High*.

One of the first records ABC-Paramount released by us was the "A-B-C Song," which was the Dixie Cups singing the children's alphabet song. The label actually tried to promote this record, because we appeared on a television show to sing it. At least we looked good singing while go-go dancers tried to act as juvenile as possible behind us. There was even a close-up of one dancer sucking on a lollipop. The Jackson Five also had a song called "ABC," but it wasn't the children's song, and it came out five years after our record. Our "A-B-C Song" never charted; the Jackson Five song was a #1 record.

ABC-Paramount also recorded a Dixie Cups tune called "What Goes Up, Must Come Down," which was written by my sister Barbara and Lee Diamond. I don't remember much about Lee, who I believe was another artist who recorded out of New Orleans. Joe must have known him. His real name was Wilbert Smith, and he wrote and sang an old-school rock 'n' roller called "Hattie Malatti" on Vee-Jay Records. I don't think "What Goes Up, Must Come Down" was ever released as a single.

The big hope for ABC-Paramount was an "Iko Iko"-type, Native American/Black American–rhythm song called "Two-Way-Poc-Away." The circumstances were similar to those of "Iko Iko." We were in the studio and just started chanting an old New Orleans rhythm. Everyone liked it, and it was recorded quickly. Barbara, Joan Marie, and I got credit for writing it, along with Harold Fedison, who helped design our Indian costumes. The record says it was arranged by Joe Jones, which is a lie. He wasn't at the session when we made that recording. The B-side was "That's Where It's At," written by Carl Hogan and Marilyn Jones. The latter was Joe's wife's name, although, of course, she didn't write the song.

It is doubtful Joe made any contribution, as he wasn't at the recording sessions, and Hogan had been writing songs since the 1940s with Louis Jordan. Hogan's guitar lead to Jordan's "Ain't That Just Like a Woman" later morphed into the intro to Chuck Berry's "Johnny B. Goode."

The New Orleans soul group the Meters, which was a funk band put together by Art Neville, took the song and reinvented it as "Hey Pocky A-Way." The Dixie Cups version has been eclipsed by this version, which has been recorded by the Grateful Dead, among many others. The interior lines in the Meters' version became more universal:

> Lie back grooving, riding in your car
> Makes no difference where you are
> Feel good music in your soul
> Makes your body do a slow boogie roll.

Big Chief Donald Harrison Jr., a New Orleans saxophonist, son of the original leader of the Guardian of the Flames Indian tribe, and the second Big Chief, preferred the Dixie Cups version, which he thought was closer to the original "Two-Way-Poc-Away," and that's because our song is more New Orleans Mardi Gras oriented.

> Two-Way Poc-Away, Two-Way-Poc-Away
> Early in the morning
> Come get the big chief
> Big chief ready.

Then it comes down to meaning. What do we mean by "Poc-Away" or, as the Meters pronounced it, Pocky-way? There is probably a specific meaning, but I just tell people the meaning is Creole/Native American talk for whatever you feel.

ABC-Paramount produced a ton of records in 1965, some by well-known singers such as B.B. King and Fats Domino, with little notice by the teenage public. Ray Charles recorded a bunch of singles in '65 that also saw no chart action. It was a fallow year for him, as it was for the company. The one big hit for the label that year was "People Get Ready" by the Impressions. Like most everything ABC-Paramount did that year, the Dixie Cups recordings barely saw sales or chart action.

That brings me back to the album *Riding High*. Released in 1965, it at least showed that the Dixie Cups were Blacks, but once again no picture of the group, just an illustration of us flying in a whimsical, hot-air balloon. I should add the illustration is not exactly flattering to us or Black people in general.

Riding High was a Joe Jones production from beginning to end. This album was all about Joe. Besides his being listed as conductor and arranger for the album, his name and pseudonyms are on almost every song. If you can find some of the 45s derived from the album, you will see on the label something called Melder Publishing Co., which was a publishing company Joe put together for himself with Dixie Cups money. I bring that up because a number of songs on the album have a cowriter named Edmund Melder, which was one of Joe's pseudonyms. So, "I'm Not the Kind of Girl (To Marry)," the fifth song on the album and B-side to the "What Comes Up, Must Come Down" 45 record, has three writers, Barbara Hawkins, Joan Johnson, and Edmund Melder. We did a version of the traditional Irish folk song "Danny Boy" for the album, and the credits read: "Arranged by Edmund Melder." That wasn't even the sneakiest thing Joe did. Listed as cowriters were family members and even Vivian Bates, who was the New Orleans singer that Joe brought to New York along with the Dixie Cups.

The final song on the A-side of the album is "I've Got to Get That Boy," written by Edmund Melder, Sharon Jones, and Vivian Bates. The same group gets credit for the fourth song on the B-side, "I'll Never Let the Well Run Dry." Among the Joneses getting credit for songs were Marilyn (wife), Deborah and Sharon (daughters). Although Joe wrote or co-opted most of the tunes on the album, Joe put his real name to only one song, "Here It Comes Again," where the cowriters are Carl Hogan, Deborah Jones, and Joseph Jones Jr.

Just to make sure that any record buyer (there weren't many, as this album did not sell) interested in this album would know who the genius was that put the album together, the back side of the album consists mostly of liner notes (common in the 1950s through 1970s) with the header, in large letters, reading "The Dixie Cups; RIDING HIGH, Conducted by JOE JONES." Only the album's name and Joe's name are all in capital letters.

Of the four paragraphs in the liner notes, the third is dedicated solely to Joe and reads: "The Dixie Cups' success is in no small part due to another talent—that of Joe Jones, their manager, who has also made a name as bandleader and recording artist in his own right. Joe, together with Wardell Quezergue, arranged the songs in this album, and the entire collection was produced by Jones."

What happened to the album? It's hard to say. Joe brought us to ABC-Paramount when it was beginning to hit corporate turbulence. By 1966 the label was renamed ABC Records. A few years later, it would move headquarters to California. In the wider music industry, there was a whole new world of sounds. The Beatles ushered in the British Invasion groups, folk-rock rose up out of the old folk music genre, and soul music was the new incarnation of the old R&B scene. In 1965, except for the Supremes (as a Motown group, now considered soul, no longer a girl group), the girl group sound was over. Of the top 100 records for that year, only the Supremes' "Stop! In the Name of Love" and "Back in My Arms Again," and Martha and the Vandellas' "Nowhere to Run" made the list. Both groups recorded for Motown or its subsidiary label. The year before, seven of the top 100 songs were by girl groups, and most of those were written by Jeff and Ellie.

The changing music scene was the least of our problems. Joe always played fast and loose with contracts where he was in the supportive (Joe under contract to another person or company) position, which was a 180-degree difference from when he held the contract on someone else. The Dixie Cups, when moved to ABC-Paramount, were legally still under contract to Red Bird. This was at a point where Joe's macho took over. His attitude was, "I'm Joe Jones, and I can do this and I can do that." As with everything about Joe, it all looked golden at the start, but then it all ended up as a lump of coal. Joe made his move, and then Red Bird made its countermove, suing Joe Jones and ABC-Paramount. The Dixie Cups were not sued; we couldn't break the contract because we were underage. Joe had authority. None of us, the Dixie Cups, were around the legal proceedings when the powers that be were deciding our fate. When it all came to a head between Red Bird, Joe Jones, and ABC-Paramount, the outcome was that Red Bird was no longer dealing with us, and ABC-Paramount was no longer dealing with us. Word gets out. Joe never got us another recording contract, because no one wanted to work with him.

As far as the recording industry was concerned, the Dixie Cups had fallen through the cracks.

In a pique and a chance for some quick cash, Joe took us to a new record label, but he was so shortsighted that he didn't realize the Dixie Cups constituted his only business, and a lawsuit from Red Bird could do us damage, which it did. The recording side of the Dixie Cups was over, and that would eventually affect the performing side. Joe shot himself in the foot and the brain.

Barbara, Joan, and I hung on as a touring act, although it gradually got more and more difficult. Agents that used to book us stopped booking us because they didn't want to deal with Joe. The agents that we had met and that knew the Dixie Cups on a personal level said to us, when you get away from Joe Jones and have your contract back in your hands, give us a call.

If we were to hang on in New York, we needed to get a job outside of being the Dixie Cups. In 1968 Barbara and I found employment in the warehouse for Spartan's Department Store, which was in one of the outer boroughs of the city. I was in the accounting department, and Barbara in another back office position. When we came in for the job, the lady looked at our application and noticed the Manhattan address. We told her we were with a singing group, and she said, "I wish you all the luck, because with the money you're going to be making here, you won't be able to keep up the rent where you're staying." She knew the building.

Somehow Joe found out where we were working and came by to see what was going on. "Oh, you got to have a job," he said, laughing at us. His visit was not purely social or even for derogatory purposes. He was desperate for funds. The next day he asked Barbara if she would give him money because he was two months behind in rent, the lights were turned off, and the landlord was threatening to put him, his girlfriend, and their kids on the street. Money was going to come in, he said to Barbara, but he was short at the moment. "I'll give it back to you in a week's time," he stammered. I said to Barbara, "I'm not going to give him a dime, and don't you dare either." She said, "But he has those children. I can't have the kids being put on the street." She broke down and gave him the money he needed. As he was walking out, he shot back, "You'll wait for this before I pay you."

This wasn't the first time Barbara bailed Joe out. One time, she saved his life.

In our building lived three white, very pretty young ladies who were dancers at the Peppermint Lounge in Manhattan. This was a clear instance of Joe not paying attention or of letting his penis instead of his brain think for him.

In the early 1960s, due to the dance craze the Twist, the Peppermint Lounge had become the hottest nightclub on the planet, packed with international celebrities and socialites. Joey Dee and the Starliters were the house band and had a #1 hit with the song "Peppermint Twist, Part 1." The Ronettes started out as dancers at the club. The downside to all this hedonistic glory was that the club was owned by mobster Johnny Biello, a member of the Genovese family.

Joe had this great idea that he was going to make the three dancers into a singing group called the Adorns—an obvious rip-off of the Dixie Cups concept, as Adorn was a consumer product, a hairspray popular with teenage girls. The young ladies were friendly and often would knock at our door, come in, and chat. They may have been good dancers, but they couldn't sing their way out of a paper bag. Joe eventually signed one of them to a contract, telling her the usual line that he was going to make her a star. He had this grand concept that with every record released by the Adorns, there would be a free can of Adorn hairspray—a promotion no one could turn down. He went to the company that made Adorn, asked for a whole lot of money, and was told, "No way, Jose." So the relationship between Joe and the girl ended up to be him just wanting her in a nonprofessional way. This went on for a while, until the girl realized she was just being played and asked Joe to give her back the contract. That was not Joe's style. A contract where Joe was the principal was sacrosanct—it was also leverage—and he strongly asserted, "I have this contract, you signed it, and I'm not giving it up." The girl didn't argue. Instead, she went back to the Peppermint Lounge and told the bosses of her problem. A few days later, there was a knock on Joe's door. He opened it up to find two big, burly guys standing there asking for the girl's contract. Joe dismissed them with an f-you. They grabbed Joe and dragged him to the window. Marion, Joe's girlfriend in New York who shared an apartment with him, ran out of the apartment, down the stairs, and into our apartment, begging us to do something because they were going to kill him. Barbara immediately scampered up to the eighth floor to Joe's apartment and went in. She found the two guys holding Joe by his heels, hanging him out the window. Please, she begged Joe, tell them where the contract is, and they'll let you go. Well, they certainly had Joe over a barrel—actually a windowsill—and he gave in. The two guys burned the contract and for good measure beat the hell out of Joe. If Barbara hadn't arrived, they would probably have let him fall.

Joan Marie had been born with sickle-cell anemia and wasn't expected to live past age fifteen. She was a real trouper, and the disease didn't physically impede her in those early Dixie Cups years. What eventually ground Joan Marie down was the traveling and Joe continually chastising and criticizing us. Finally she just couldn't take the presence of him in her life anymore.

In 1966 the Dixie Cups were on another tour. We had just finished our set and came off the stage. One of the road managers immediately came up to us and said you need to call your manager very quickly. We thought, Oh, something is wrong with one of our parents. We couldn't get Joe, so then we started thinking maybe something was going on with him, and if that was the case, then we didn't care that much. Barbara said, "What do we need to call him for?" Then either Joan Marie or I suggested we call back Joe's friend and bandmate, trumpet player Melvin Lastie, who was the person who called us about Joe. Barbara telephoned, with Joan and me trying to listen in on the receiver. Melvin started to stutter, which he did when he got nervous. "They got my boy shackled hands and feet, and he's going to be on that van headed to Rikers Island" (where the prison was located). "What for?" Barbara asked. Melvin explained that Joe had amassed parking tickets all over New York and never paid one of them. The police had put out a warrant for him, and when they got him, he couldn't talk his way out. He kept telling the police that the women who had his money were on tour, and as soon as they came back he would pay the tickets. The police slipped the cuffs on him and said, "Off you go." That's when Melvin made his call.

Joan Marie and I asked how much Joe was in arrears. Melvin told us. I can't remember the amount anymore, but it was astronomical. Melvin asked, "I know this is not a payday, but do you think the tour will allow you all to get a draw?"

Joan and I said to Barbara, "Don't pay it," but she went to the tour manager, who gave her our remittance in advance.

That year Joan Marie finally threw in the towel, partly because of the disease but mostly because of the mess Joe was taking us through. What was the last straw? One evening we were in our apartment, and Joe came through the door in a foul temper. He made himself comfortable and, as usual, started badmouthing us, calling us one foul name after another. Joan Marie looked up and said to him, "Shut up. I'm tired of hearing your mouth." When he didn't stop, she picked up a box of records and poured the contents over the top of his head. Then she went into the bedroom, called her parents to send her some money for airfare, and started packing her clothes. She was gone within two days.

Barbara (in white dress), mother (Lucille Cordelia Merette Hawkins), and Rosa (about seven years old). Photo taken in their New Orleans home.

Lucille Hawkins with guitarist (name unknown) from the Papa Celestin band.

Rosa at about eight years of age.

Lucille Cordelia Merette Hawkins with her mother, also named Cordelia Merette.

INSIDE NEW ORLEANS

SATURDAY, JUNE 26, 1965

You'll notice that the people who really keep up with local events in the world of education read TOTS AND TEENS each week in Inside New Orleans. They read it because they have come to know that Lucille Hawkins consistently reports, item for item, significant events.

Mrs. Hawkins has become a familiar figure in the world of education. Whether it is a cotillion or a news conference with the U. S. Commissioner of Education, Francis Kepell, you are almost certain to find Mrs. Hawkins there. She is alert and busy gathering items they will make you and your children better informed readers.

Make it a point that you and your family read Mrs. Hawkins' reports during the summer months. She will make it profitable indeed.

If you are not already receiving Inside New Orleans at home, we'll be happy to deliver it to you every week. Simply phone 943–3393 ... ask for Circulation.

Inside
NEW ORLEANS 
ONLY NEWSPAPER READERS GET ALL THE NEWS

lucille hawkins reports education

Lucille Hawkins and her local newspaper column "Inside New Orleans," 1965.

Lucille Hawkins (second from left, middle row) with the Pastor's Aid Club in New Orleans.

The original Dixie Cups in 1965, with Joan Marie Johnson.

The original Dixie Cups on tour in Vietnam.

On tour in Vietnam.

The Dixie Cups

The Dixie Cups are a talented young group of singers. Barbara Ann Hawkins, Joan Johnson and Rosa Lee Hawkins are originally from New Orleans and have been singing professionally for a short time. The Dixie Cups made their first recording, "Chapel of Love", one year ago this February. It was released in March of 1964.

The Dixie Cups follow-up was "People Say", which went to No. 4 in the nation; the third was, "You Should Have Seen The Way He Looked At Me", and the fourth and current release, "Little Bell", is riding high. The Dixie Cups "Chapel of Love" was the first so-called Rock 'n' Roll album to go into the Columbia Record Club. They were presented with two gold records, "Chapel of Love" and "People Say" on the Shindig show in November.

Program from one of the many military base shows where the Dixie Cups performed.

Personal Direction
JOE JONES
(212) 246-8798
N. Y., N. Y.

THE DIXIECUPS

Exclusively Owned By
SHEDEB MANAGEMENT, INC.
300 W. 55 St.   N. Y., N. Y.

This photo was used as the cover for the *Iko Iko* album. (Notice lower left; Joe Jones was the group's manager at this time.)

THE SWINGIN' SOUNDS
STARS OF THE MONTH ... THE DIXIE CUPS

Three little girls from Southern University in New Orleans, the Dixie Cups, became VIPs on campus when their very first record, Chapel of Love on the Red Bird label, climbed to the No. 1 position on every popularity chart in the country. As a group, Rosa Lee and Barbara Ann Hawkins and Joan Marie Johnson have been singing together almost a year now, although their individual careers started long ago in elementary school.

Their present manager, Joe Jones, found them in an amateur talent show and brought the girls to New York in an attempt to get them started on a recording career. Making the rounds, they finally came to the offices of Jerry Leiber and Mike Stoller, who already have a long established reputation for writing and producing hit records.

Jerry and Mike listened to the girls sing, and within 24 hours the recording contracts were signed, studio time was booked, and the newly-christened "Dixie Cups" were rehearsing Chapel of Love for their first recording session. Less than a month later, the record was released on the brand-new Red Bird label.

The girls are still overwhelmed by their sudden thrust into nationwide popularity, but they haven't forgotten the level foundations afforded them by strong family ties and education. They still like the things they always liked, and spend what little spare time they have in reading to continue their education, or in furthering their talent in primitive art, their favorite hobby.

Once in a while, when they can get away from rehearsals and studios and road trips long enough, they even manage to get outdoors for a day of sun, swimming and sports. It's a good thing all three Dixie Cups are also crazy about traveling, for that's what they seem to be doing most these days.

THE DIXIE CUPS

Story about the Dixie Cups in *Sepia* magazine. Year unknown.

Being interviewed on a United Kingdom television show.

With the London executives of Red Bird Records.

Personal Direction
JOE JONES
(212) 246-8798
N. Y., N. Y.

THE DIXIECUPS

Exclusively Owned By
SHEDEB MANAGEMENT, INC.
300 W. 55 St.   N. Y., N. Y.

Another photo taken at the *Iko Iko* album cover shoot.

Photo taken while the girls were singing on a United Kingdom television show.

Performing on a cruise ship. The third Dixie Cup (on left) is Dale Mickle.

NFL GAMEDAY

New Orleans SAINTS

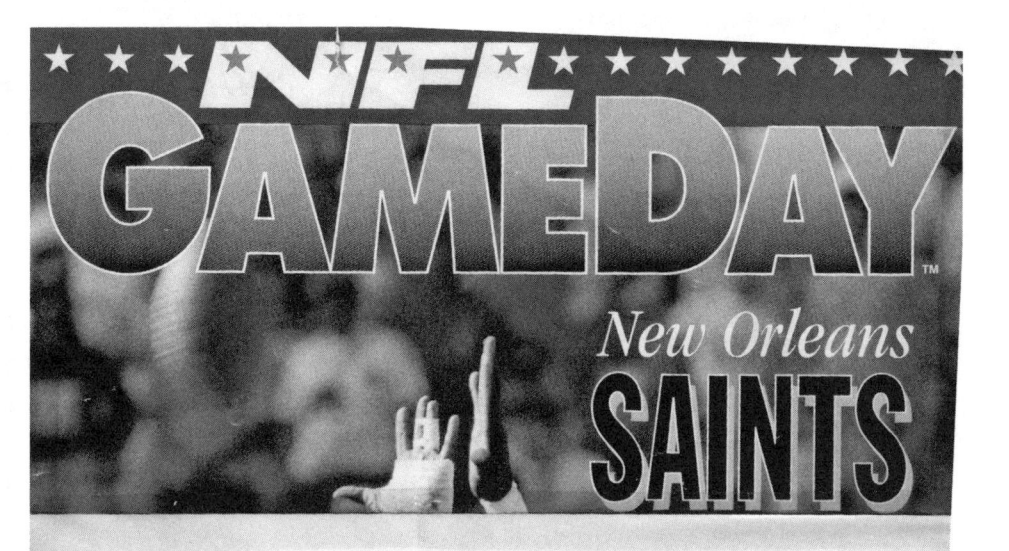

SPONSORED BY KENTWOOD SPRING WATER

January 2, 1994

Today's Entertainment

PREGAME SHOW
The New Orleans Acro-Gymnastic School
Directed by Jurek Pol

COLOR GUARD
Jesuit High School Junior Marine ROTC
under the supervision of
Mst./Sgt. Lary Abshire

SMOKEY BEAR
will be our special guest at today's game. He is celebrating his 50th year as America's famous symbol of forest fire prevention.

REMEMBER...
SMOKEY HAS FOR FIFTY YEARS

THE DIXIE CUPS
The Star-Spangled Banner will be sung this afternoon by one of New Orleans best known singing groups ... The Dixie Cups. With hit recordings such as "Chapel of Love", "People Say", "Iko-Iko" and "Little Bell", the trio of Barbara A. Hawkins, Rosa B. Hawkins and Dale T. Mickle have appeared on The Today Show, Dick Clark's American Bandstand, Showtime, Nashville Now, and in concert throughout the U.S.

SAINTS CHEERLEADERS	SAINTS AUDIO	SAINTSATIONS	FIELD ANNOUNCER	SAINTS ENTERTAINMENT ASSISTANTS
Darlene Bonis Director	Produced by Mark Coudrain	Sylvia Alfortish – Director Sandra Labourdette – Choreographer	Jim Clarke	Benny Recatto Judy Recatto Al Demarest

SAINTS vs. BENGALS	January 2, 1994 Louisiana Superdome	$3.00

Program for New Orleans Saints game in 1994. The Dixie Cups sang the national anthem.

Photo taken by local photographer at the Hawkins home in New Orleans. Third Dixie Cup is Beverly Brown.

Rosa Hawkins singing at the Lil Darlin's Rock 'n' Roll Palace in Kissimmee, Florida.

Photo taken at Bread for the World charity event, early 1990s. Third Dixie Cup is Dale Mickle.

Barbara and Rosa Hawkins with author Steve Bergsman, 2019.

CHAPTER SEVEN

The House of the Rising Sun

When the Dixie Cups hit the big time with a #1 record, not only did Dick Clark book us on his upcoming Caravan of Stars tour, but he featured us along with other singers and groups who could boast big hits in 1964—along with a couple of girl group veterans.

The booking was actually done by the William Morris Agency Inc., where Joe Jones turned for professional help. The letter that came to us was very formal:

> Please be advised that the rehearsal for the show will be held on Thursday, June 25th (1964) at Nola Studios, 111 West 57th Street, in the third floor rehearsal hall, at 10 am. The bus will be leaving on Friday, June 26th, at 12 noon, from the Park Sheraton Hotel, 56th Street and 7th Avenue . . . we will be leaving early enough to accommodate those who feel they might need extra rehearsal time. Mr. Ed McAdams will be your road manager.

Ironically, the letter from William Morris was more professional than the promotion. The flyer for the show was hastily conceived, with the words "The Summer Shower of Stars" in unadorned block letters at the center and surrounded by black-and-white photos of the headliners as if they were numbers on a watch face. At the one o'clock position was a vertical photo of the Shirelles, girl group superstars who had their last big hits in 1963 and became an inadvertent victim of the British Invasion when, in 1964, the English band Manfred Mann covered a B-song of theirs, "Sha-La-La," and made it a Top 20 hit. Then, moving clockwise, came photos of: the Rip Chords ("Hey Little Cobra)," which peaked at #4 on the *Billboard* charts in 1964); the Reflections ("Just Like Romeo and Juliet," which peaked at #6 on the *Billboard* charts in 1964); the Dixie Cups; Gene Pitney ("It Hurts to Be in Love," which peaked at #7 on the *Billboard* charts in 1964); and at prime position, or the twelve o'clock hour on the watch face, came the Crystals ("He's A Rebel," a #1 hit in 1962, "Da Doo Ron Ron," a #2 hit in 1963, "Then He Kissed Me," a #6 record in 1963, but no major hits in 1964).

When the caravan bus pulled out of the East Coast and headed for the first stop at Allentown, Pennsylvania, before swinging north to Hartford, Connecticut, the other performers on the caravan were Dean and Jean, Mike Clifford, Brenda Holloway, Brian Hyland, the Kasuals, Major Lance, George McCannon, Round Robin, and the Supremes. The latter group started out on the show's B-positions, but after scoring a #1 record in the summer of 1964 with "Where Did Our Love Go," they also became headliners.

I just want to pass a little love and thanks to the Shirelles, because they had been on the road off and on for the prior years and knew what they were doing even before they boarded the bus for a Dick Clark tour. Prior to the tour, the Shirelles took us under their wing, because they saw we were three young ladies who didn't know what we were getting into. They brought us to different wig places in Harlem, because, once again, we were novices. I had never worn a wig in my life, and neither had Barbara and Joan Marie. We didn't know we needed wigs. Barbara's beautiful hair was down to her shoulders and of a soft texture.

LaRay Valdee, our beautician, was a makeup artist for several cosmetic lines. He taught me how to apply makeup, and I passed this knowledge on to Barbara and Joan Marie. LaRay had a shop in Harlem and often traveled, doing makeup for different performers and stars. He was a sweetheart.

Money always came to Joe first, unless he wasn't there. For the Caravan of Stars Tour, he wasn't included, but every now and then he would fly out to where we were so he could get our pay first. The first time Joe showed up, Dick Clark called Barbara to his room and asked if he should give the money to Joe, and Barbara said yes, he is our manager. The arrangement for us was, when Joe got back to New York City, he would pay all our bills. He would also leave us spending money. Since Barbara was the leader of the group, he would do all of the dealings with Barbara. If we were on the road, with our modest spending cash, all the girls would go shopping. Barbara would give Joan and me money, and the three of us would meet with girls from the Shirelles or the Supremes, and we would all do a shopping day.

One time all the singing groups were on one bus, while the instruments, uniforms, and gowns were on another vehicle. That bus did not make it to the arena on time. Dick Clark came to the dressing room and asked to speak to us. "Listen," he said, "you know the bus is not here with everyone's outfits. Would you all mind if the Supremes could use one of your outfits for the show because theirs are on the other bus?" We had our clothes with us, and Florence Ballard was the same size as Joan Marie, a little bit heavy, so that worked out. Mary Wilson was the same size as me, tall and skinny. And Diana was the same waist size as Barbara; the only difference was Barbara was shorter than Diana. Mary and Florence said of course we'll wear their outfits, but Diana said no. So she called Berry Gordy, who then spoke with Dick Clark. That night the Supremes went on stage with the clothes they had put on that morning at the hotel.

After that we did some extracurricular things together with the Supremes, except for Diana, who didn't want to go shopping with us. Mary Wilson and Dolores "Dee Dee" Kenniebrew of the Crystals were very close friends to us. To this day I still keep in contact with both of them.

Mostly, I read to pass the time on the bus. Joan Marie would crack jokes. Our first tormentors in good fun were the singing duo Dean and Jean, in real life Welton Young and Brenda Lee Jones from Ohio. They were great singers and guitarists—very professional on stage. Offstage, they were funny and annoying in equal measure. I can still recall being on the bus: I'm on one seat with a book in my hand, Barbara is sitting with a pillow under her head trying to go to sleep, and Joan Marie is trying to think of a rebuttal to Dean and Jean, who were picking on her. Dean and Jean started recording around 1958 and spent the following six years under the radar, never quite making the charts in any substantial way. So, they were veterans of the circuit and glad to be on the Dick Clark tour. They had seen it all from inside the bus and took it upon themselves to break in the newbies like the Dixie Cups. They decided we were such nice girls, in fact three young ladies who were too nice and too polite for a bus full of entertainers. They would plant themselves behind us, and when one of us would fall asleep, Jean would start to jokingly ramble, "Oh yeah, those Dixie Cups, they don't say any bad words. Y'all don't say anything like 'Get the hell out of my face.'" She would do this whispering. If we smiled, then she would say, "We're going to get y'all before you get off this trip. Y'all are going to be saying four-letter words. It will be words you never said before." They would whisper words that if my mama ever heard me using them, I would be dead. Dean and Jean were so funny. They didn't mean any harm and didn't use foul words in a nasty way. Dick Clark once said to them, "Why don't you leave the girls alone?" and Jean answered, "Nah, you put them on this here bus, and I got to ingrain them, because when they go on the next tour, they are not going to have Dean and me here to take care of them."

Gene Pitney, one of the headliners on the tour, was also kind of an instigator. He used to sit in the back of the bus all the time, often starting rumors. He might say something innocuous like "Bad news spreads like wildfire," and everybody would go, "What, what's the bad news?" Then he would say, "I don't have none, I was waiting for someone to add to it." He did funny things like that. Gene was a total gentleman, a lovable person, and real talent as a singer and songwriter. He started recording in 1958 and by 1963 had written such great songs as "Town without Pity," "(The Man Who Shot) Liberty Valance," and "Only Love Can Break a Heart." He was also a Brill Building guy, writing "He's a Rebel" for the Crystals and "Hello Mary Lou" for Ricky Nelson.

Gene's big problem was the Dixie Cups, because Dick Clark scheduled us to appear right before him—and we were hot, hot, hot on stage. For that tour we had matching gold jumpsuits, tight slacks, and spangled, revealing tank tops with spaghetti straps. Once we cranked up "Chapel of Love," "People Say," and "Iko Iko," the audience would call us back, yelling for more. One time we were standing backstage after our set, and Gene was about to go on. He turned to Dick Clark and said, "Dick, they are killing me." Dick questioned, "Who is killing who?" And Gene said, "The Cups. I can't walk out there." The audience was still screaming for us. Gene shook his head. "Look how long it's taking just to get the audience quiet." Dick nodded to Jimmy O'Neil, who as master of ceremonies went to calm them down and introduce Gene.

We found the situation funny, because we had just gotten into the music industry, and this was our first tour. We did not know or understand what it meant to have an act go on right before you and that act was so good, the audience liked the songs so well, they weren't ready to see the next star. One time Dick told us to go back out and sing the last part of "Chapel of Love," which we did. Then we thanked the audience and went off. Jimmy quickly went onto the stage and introduced Gene Pitney. Like passing a hot potato, they immediately passed their affections onto Gene and forgot about the Dixie Cups.

Major Lance, who was on a roll with three big hits in a row ("The Monkey Time," "Hey Little Girl," and "Um Um Um Um Um Um") was on the tour. He was extremely afraid of trains, and that bit of learned knowledge by the other performers just rattled through the bus, because we had to cross a track somewhere in the Midwest. The driver, Willie, knew everything going on with everybody on the bus except the Dixie Cups, because we were new to everyone; we were the only ones who hadn't done a prior tour on that bus.

Willie was talking to Paul Peterson ("My Dad," a Top 10 record in 1962), giving him advance warning that we had some train tracks coming up in a half hour. Willie whispered, "We have to do our routine," and Paul said, "I'll do it, because last time he almost had a real heart attack." Everyone on the bus knew what they were talking about except us. We had to ask what was going on. We found out fairly quickly because, as we were about to cross the railroad tracks, everyone started making train-on-tracks noises, including the whistle. Major Lance woke up and said to his seatmate, "What's wrong with the bus?" and the guy said, "I don't know, Major. It is stuck, and I can't open the doors." When Major would get upset, he would repeat his words a lot. Everyone on the bus was yelling to hit the brakes, and Willie yelled back, "I hit the brakes about ninety-two times." Major yelled, "Open the back door so I can go out!" The driver answered that none of the doors would open, because they were all electric. Major was so afraid, he started cursing, but his curse words weren't coming out as cursing because he was too scared. When he saw some of us laughing, he caught on. "Goddammit," he yelled. "This bus wasn't stopped on no tracks. Open this goddam bus so I can get off." Everyone on the bus was rolling. Finally, Willie said, "Wait, Major, I'm trying," and he would make the engine grind like it was stuck. Finally he got it going. As soon as the bus stopped, Major opened the door and jumped out. The Dixie Cups were laughing so hard, and Major said, "See these little innocent girls, they don't know nothing about what you all are doing, and you are turning them against me." We said, "We aren't against you. We're just laughing because there was no train." Major Lance was a real trip.

By July 13 when the caravan rolled into Pittsburgh to play the Syria Mosque, a popular venue, the Supremes pushed past the Shirelles as headliners, and the show got smaller, with Bobby Freeman joining the tour, and the Crystals, Brenda Holloway, George McCannon, and the Kasuals leaving. After a show in Cincinnati on July 18, the Shirelles and the Supremes left the tour.

The caravan rolled through the Midwest to the Pacific and then back to the East Coast. The Dixie Cups stayed with it until the end. It was a killer tour. On September 4 the tour hit Green Bay, Wisconsin, and then, finally, the last stop on September 7 at Conneaut Lake Park, Pennsylvania.

This last show venue was located in western Pennsylvania, less than two hours' driving time from Cleveland. We were exhausted and wanting to go home as quickly as possible, so we decided to fly back to New York, expecting Joe to pick us up in his car, which he kept ready and at our expense in Manhattan. Arriving back in the Big Apple, we recovered our luggage and looked around for Joe. He wasn't there. Thankfully, we had enough money between us for a taxi.

The Dixie Cups lived in Manhattan at 200 West Fifty-Fifth Street, sharing apartment 4E like it was a dormitory. After one more tortuous ride through crosstown traffic, we, joyous young ladies, and now trunk-tour veterans, were finally home. We gathered our luggage, which we pulled, pushed, and dragged into the apartment building, took the elevator to the fourth floor, repeated all the pushing and pulling, and got to our door to find a big orange notification attached saying something to the effect that since the rent hadn't been paid, there was to be no access. We looked at each other thinking, What the hell is this all about? We tried the key, but the lock had been changed or blocked. "This can't be, because all our money has been sent to Joe since we've been on the road," Barbara offered despondently. We left our bags and looked for Joe, who lived on the eighth floor, but he wasn't around. So we took the orange paper down to the office, where we discovered the rent hadn't been paid in three months, and we were to be evicted.

The manager of the apartment building liked us, realized we were in a situation not of our own making, and allowed us to get back into the apartment pending a discussion with Joe Jones. But, having observed Joe Jones as a tenant, he warned us. "I keep an eye on you ladies, and you really need to get away from that man. He is not doing you all any good."

The Dixie Cups didn't take the warning seriously. Joe Jones was our manager, my legal guardian because I was underage, and we trusted him, even if the immediate situation continued to spiral away from us. We were given access to the apartment only to discover there was no electricity. And the phone was turned off. Those bills weren't paid either. There was also no food in the pantry, apparently because Joe, his mistress, and his kids were eating in our apartment when we were gone.

Eventually Joe Jones returned, entering the apartment on his own because he had keys. We rushed at him, expressing anger, confusion, and disappointment, all easy emotions for Joe to deflect. He had his excuses lined up, apologizing and saying the money had to be used for photographs and to get music written, and the car needed some work. It was an error and wouldn't happen again. As we were later to learn, except for the car, the money we earned was sent to New Orleans because all his children there were in private school and the bills came due. In addition, his perennially neglected house in Louisiana was about to collapse into a heap of wood and stone. It had to be rebuilt, and the contractor wanted his dollars.

Joe settled with the apartment manager, who realized we were in a tough situation and told us when we go out of town again, he knew what to do with Joe, and he would make certain our rent would be paid.

That going out of town came quickly.

Less than a year before, we had never been out of the Deep South, never beyond the borders of Louisiana and Mississippi. Now we were living in Manhattan and had just concluded a cross-country tour. Life was exciting, and it was about to get even more thrilling, as the William Morris Agency was putting us on a tour of England. Joe had farmed out some of his agent duties to the bigger organization from the start of our career. When Joe came around to tell us William Morris would again be booking another tour, we were thrilled, especially when we were told not only would we be going to England, but we would be booked on British television with *Ready Steady Go!*, a teen- and preteen-oriented show that debuted on August 9, 1963. Earlier in 1963 the show garnered its highest ratings in its four-year history when the Beatles were guest stars, singing three songs and sitting for a quick interview. In America a similar show called *Shindig!* didn't debut until September 1964, although Dick Clark's *American Bandstand* had been around since the 1950s.

On October 30, 1964, the Dixie Cups sang their latest hit, "People Say." Also appearing on the show were the Kinks, singing "All Day and All of the Night," and a Filipino American singer named Sugar Pie DeSanto, who had a #4 R&B hit in 1960 with "I Want to Know." She was touring with the American Folk Blues Festival in 1964 and came on the show to sing "I Don't Wanna Fuss."

I kept a sharp eye on the female competition, not so much the British bands, because there were just too many. At the time I didn't know who the Kinks were. What I do remember was that Dusty Springfield was a big deal in England at the time. Indeed, Dusty was having a banner year in 1964, with "I Only Want to Be with You," "Wishin' and Hopin'," and "I Just Don't Know What to Do with Myself" all charting strongly in the US and the UK. She was in such demand that the Dixie Cups' appearance on *Ready Steady Go!* was sandwiched between her appearance on the show the week before with Gene Pitney and the week after with a monster lineup of the Dave Clark Five, Marianne Faithful, Sandy Shaw, and the Rolling Stones.

On one tour to England, we played with the Rolling Stones. We also met the Beatles. This was at the Ad Lib Club at 7 Leicester Place in London, a special club where many of the British singers would end up late at night. We didn't know it at the time, but as one journalist wrote, it was a "hangout for pop-stars such as The Stones and The Kinks, actors and actresses, fashionistas and even Princess Margaret. The music policy was exclusively black American soul and blues records and the door policy was even stricter."

What happened was that Paul McCartney was at one of our London appearances and after the show came backstage to visit. He greeted us by saying, "I'm Paul of the Beatles." After the greetings, I remember telling him we were famished, and he said, "If you want to get something to eat, there is a club just for recording artists, and I'd like to bring you over." He was very polite. There was another man with him, probably security, and this gentleman offered: "I'll take them there." Paul went into a lead car, and we followed. When we got to the AdLib Club, security guarded the door, but of course we were with Paul and went right in. Then it was up a flight of stairs, where there was more security. Again we went right in. Some of the guys from the Rolling Stones and the Animals were already there. We had played on the same show with the Rolling Stones but never formally met. Mick Jagger stepped forward, shook our hands, and said, "We like your music." Then he found us three seats and asked, "Want a drink?" He could not have been sweeter.

A long communal table was the key bit of furniture in the room. It was already past midnight, and what was most important to the Dixie Cups was that you could order breakfast if that was what you wanted to eat. It was complimentary if you ordered drinks. When we got to the table, the Rolling Stones were on one end, and the Beatles were in the middle. Brian Hyland was on this leg of the tour, and he was with us—we were the only females in the room. When we got to the table, Paul stood up and wanted to introduce everyone. The Beatles hadn't met us, but we knew the Rolling Stones and the Animals. One of the Rolling Stones, I think it was Brian Jones, went into the bathroom and locked himself in one of the stalls and was crying. Paul was good friends with the Stones, and one of them asked Paul if he could come and help him get Brian out of the bathroom. "Why won't he come out?" Paul asked. "Because you introduced the Dixie Cups to everyone at the table, but you didn't call his name," was the answer. Paul said, "You already knew them; you were on a bill together." The Stone said, "That's not the same thing," avoiding the obvious, that Brian was sky-high on something. So Paul got one of the other Beatles and went to the bathroom. By this time the line for the men's room was getting long. They didn't want everyone in the club to know what was going on. They kept saying, "C'mon, man, you got to come out, you got people waiting." When Brian came out, Paul put his arm around him, directed him to the table, and said, "And these are the Dixie Cups, and Dixie Cups this is Brian Jones." No one thought twice about why he had locked himself in the bathroom. He said, "I'm sorry I had to leave the table, but my stomach was a little upset." We sat in that place all night; I didn't know I could stay up that late.

Being from the South, we liked sunny-side-up eggs that we would cook on both sides. When Barbara gave the waiter-manager at the late-night club our order, he looked confused. "What's sunny-side up?" he asked, scratching his head, "I don't know what you are saying." Barbara said, "I can come in the kitchen and show you exactly what it is." I thought to myself, Oh no, not again, because Barbara would go in anybody's kitchen and do whatever just to get the food the way she wanted. She went in the kitchen, got everyone's order, and cooked up the eggs. One of the guys at the table said, "I have never seen him let anyone in his kitchen, and there she is fixing her eggs the way she wanted."

The waiter-manager asked, "What do you usually eat with this?" Barbara said, "We eat grits." And he laughed, "Grits. What is grits?" Barbara said, "I'll send you a package." We all had hash browns instead. That night Joe Jones was not with us. We enjoyed ourselves and had a wonderful time with everyone we met.

I was a collector of names, phone numbers, and birth dates. I liked to send birthday and thank-you cards. I sent cards to Paul McCartney and Mick Jagger.

On another tour we worked with the original Coasters. Cornell Gunter came to our room in England because we were freezing; we weren't used to that type of heating system, where to get heat you had to insert money, a shilling, for the machine to turn on. Then it seemed as if the heat would only last three seconds. Gunter showed us how to manipulate the coin box to make sure the room stayed comfortable without continued contributions. Every night the service guy would empty the box of money. When he opened the box and found only one or two shillings, he looked at us and asked, "You're not cold; it was such and such degrees last night." We said we were from the South, that's what we were used to.

Our room at the hotel, which today is The Rubens at the Palace, was opposite the gates of Buckingham Palace. We would watch the changing of the guard. We didn't see the queen, only the queen's coach.

The Dixie Cups felt blessed to be traveling out of the country for the first time. Joe, who was part of the travel package put together by the promoter, decided to make a holiday out of it for himself and invited his wife to join the party. Her expenses, of course, came out of the proceeds from the group's earnings. We didn't quite understand this but remained kindly and respectful to Marilyn Jones. We loved the woman we called Mrs. Jones. She was a congenial lady who treated us well, always asking about our families back in New Orleans. She was a nice person who was trying to raise her family as best she could with her husband in New York. She wasn't stupid and knew her husband wasn't faithful, but as long as Joe paid the bills and treated her right when they were together, she was fine with her life. Saving us any discomfort, Mrs. Jones never asked us one personal question about her husband.

Joan Marie and I were still teenagers and, like many in this age bracket, had to deal with profound insecurities while at the same time trying to appear to be grownup. Small things mean a lot to young adults, and no one likes to be made fun of, but Joe knew how to stick the knife in, and that first trip to Europe ended with hurt feelings.

Each of us had her own combination of Samsonite, including a makeup case. Once we arrived at the airport, the porter placed our makeup cases behind us without informing us. The lobby was crowded with entertainment reporters and photographers for a last shot at us. I stepped back to go and ask Barbara a question, neglecting to look down to see where the makeup case was. My foot landed on the case, and I began to tumble, instinctively reaching out. On my way down, I grabbed Joan Marie by her arm. The speed and mass of the fall pulled down Joan Marie, who ended up on top of me on the floor. Photographers had a field day taking pictures. I was embarrassed, Joan Marie angry, and everyone else laughing uproariously. Joe wouldn't let it go. Every time he would see me or Joan Marie walk by, he would say, "Watch where you're going, Rosa." Or, "Watch where you're going, Joan Marie." The fall itself was embarrassing enough, but the continued cruelty of Joe's remarks bothered me profoundly, as I was still, to my marrow, an overly sensitive teenager.

Joe had a shopping compulsion, which caused him serious problems when the Dixie Cups returned to England in 1967 for another tour. This time it was just Joe and the three Dixie Cups. All went fine, and the Dixie Cups and Joe ended the trip with a shopping spree in London. The next day we took a taxi to the airport.

All four of us were sitting at the airport when two men in trench coats and hats walked up. They looked like two detectives from Scotland Yard. It turns out they were.

One of the two men looked to Joe and politely asked, "Are you Joe Jones?" Joe, caught by surprise, responded curtly, "Yeah, that's me. Watcha want?" The two men in trench coats looked at each other and then turned back to Joe. "We're from Scotland Yard. You need to come with us, as you are under arrest."

Joe sputtered and rattled on, saying he didn't do anything, but the two men didn't budge and insinuated the situation could become more difficult if he didn't come with them. We panicked. "You're taking our manager to jail?" we asked. "You can't do that. What are we going to do?"

It turned out Joe had been writing bad checks all over London. He didn't go to one store to do this; he went to every store. The total amount of dollars was huge. He even bought three trunks to put all the purchases into so that he could ship it all separately to New Orleans. Once again, this was all on company checks. It wasn't even his money he was spending.

Joe had been paid the money the Dixie Cups earned on the tour, so he had the cash to pay his bills. Why didn't he? The story he initially told us was that he thought he could make it back to the States in time to put money in the bank account to cover the checks before anyone tried to cash them out. What eventually came out was that he had a lot of bills to pay in New York and thought he could just write checks and get out of town before anyone realized there was nothing in the company bank account to support the checks. He would be safe in New York, beyond the legal arm of the Brits, and to hell with the stores that got stiffed. He didn't care about who got cheated.

He always thought white shop owners owed him, because white people always exploited Black people.

At that moment in the London airport, we didn't know any of this, and I was on the verge of tears. One of the men told us we could continue on to the United States, but we were so stupidly loyal we didn't want to leave without Joe. "Do you know anyone here in London?" one of the guys asked, and Barbara said we knew a few people who were friends. "If you don't want to fly home without your manager, and you have connections, then give them a call right now and find out if you can stay with them until this matter is resolved."

Since 1964 and the coming of the Beatles, multi-act tours rolling across the United States usually included British Invasion bands. Before coming to London, the Dixie Cups had toured with the Animals, consistent hitmakers since their version of "The House of the Rising Sun" went to #1 in the States in the autumn of 1964. We girls got along well with the Londoners and made friends with the whole band, Chas Chandler, John Steel, Alan Price, Hilton Valentine, and lead singer Eric Burdon.

After the US tour, Eric gave me his London telephone number and told me if we were ever in England to give him a call. Checking our phone books, we still had telephone numbers for all of the group members. I called Eric first, but there was no answer, so I called Hilton, who picked up the phone. He remembered the Dixie Cups right away, asking how we all were. I said we needed to talk to Eric, who, as luck would have it, was there with Hilton. Eric came on the line, and I explained what was happening, that we were stuck at the airport, that Joe had all our money and we had none—literally no money between the three of us. I was crying, saying we didn't know what to do.

And Eric stepped up like a true British gentleman. The first thing he told me was to just calm down, that we could go to his flat, that I had the right address in hand, and to just tell the taxi driver where to go. I said, "Eric, we don't have any money." He said, "Don't worry about that. Find cab with number XXXX, and when you see the driver, tell him you're with me and need to go to my place. He will bring you to my address. The key is under the flowerpot outside. Find it, open the door, go in, and just relax. There is food in my house, just make yourselves at home. Eat whatever you want."

"What should we do about Joe?" I exclaimed, forever and stupidly loyal like a beaten dog. "This is what *I'm* going to do," he said. "I'm going to telephone my attorney, and he will go to Scotland Yard to meet with Joe."

We arrived at Eric Burdon's flat not knowing what to expect. Eric's flat was clean, orderly, and well designed.

We hadn't eaten since early in the morning, so we made ourselves some scrambled eggs. The only coffee was instant, which we had never seen before.

We all came from New Orleans, which in the 1960s, decades before the advent of Starbucks, was probably one of the few cities in the country where coffee brewing was an art. We grew up on fresh coffee. My grandmother would grind those beans every morning. The instant coffee was so unusual for us, we were thinking about putting some in an envelope and bringing it back to our mom.

We had no luggage, so after showering we put on some of Eric's shirts. Then we settled down and waited to find out what happened to our manager. Later in the day, Eric's attorney came by the house and told us not to worry, that everything would turn out OK. "I'm going to get Joe tomorrow at about seven o'clock in the morning, but the whole process could take all day," he said. "We don't want you ladies there. I don't need you there, as it will just cause complications. I suggest you try to make reservations to leave, not tomorrow, but the day after."

The loyal Dixie Cups decided we should call Marion, Joe's mistress in New York, and tell her what was going on. It wasn't that Marion was such a nice person, and she certainly was not friendly to us, but if she was expecting all of us on such and such a day and we didn't show up, that would be of concern to her. We would do her a kindness. Barbara made the call, with Joan and me listening in. It was no surprise that Marion immediately started cursing us, blaming us for Joe's situation, echoing Joe's opinion of us, exclaiming that we were worse than people who lived on the street. After letting her mouth off, Barbara cut in and said that first of all, Joe had all the money in his pockets and still gave out bad checks. And secondly, everything he bought, the three trunks full of clothes and doodads, were all going to his family in New Orleans and not to her in New York. That shut her up.

In the universe of Joe Jones, the expression "no good deed goes unpunished" wasn't just a throwaway line, it was the rule of law. We were taught respect, kindness, and loyalty, and it was just those traits that Joe could take advantage of. I didn't know it, but I was going to be the one punished for Joe's current misdeed.

The attorney brought Joe to Eric's apartment, and he entered, not like a criminal but like a conquering hero. As soon as the attorney left, we expected him to tell us what happened. Instead, he complained that he was hungry, he wanted something to eat. Like servants we kicked into gear with Joan Marie scrambling some eggs. All the while, he told us all about the court system in England, including how officials of the court wore wigs. He explained that the attorney Eric sent really knew his stuff. In short, he told us everything he wanted us to know without saying anything about what we wanted to know—why he was kiting bad checks.

When we told him we had called Marion, Joe flipped out, screaming, "Why did you do that?" Barbara responded, "We were just trying to keep her in the loop." So he pressed on with "Well, I hope you didn't tell her what happened with all the money and all the shopping." Barbara said, "Yes, we did." Then Joe got angry all over again, which at that point was just noise to us. For everything we did, we just didn't care anymore about Joe's anger and theatrics.

After cleaning up and calming down, it was now late in the evening. Eric had a big, king-size bed, which the three of us girls all shared. Joan Marie on one side, Barbara in the middle, and me on the other side. Joe was to sleep on the couch. It was a long, emotional two days, and we three girls were tired and fell asleep quickly and soundly.

At some point in the night, I felt somebody pushing against me. It was Joe. He was whispering, "Push over."

"What do you want?"

"I want to sleep here. It's cold in the other room."

"Well, go sleep on the floor."

He got pissed off, and we had words—all in a whisper. Barbara and Joan were soundly asleep. Joe decided to just push on the bed. I pushed him off, but he climbed back in and forcibly moved me over and grabbed me roughly, pulling up my sleeping shirt. He did what he wanted to do with me.

I was just out of high school when we came north to New York. I really never even had a boyfriend. I had a date to my prom, but it wasn't as if we were really tight. Not only was I a virgin, I never even watched these kinds of sexual situations at the movies or on television. I was so naive I didn't even realize that what was happening to me was rape.

Eric's attorney, who was a real upright gentleman, called to say he was swinging by before we left town. Barbara took the call and told him what happened with the airline, including the extra fee we would have to pay for canceling the other flight and taking a new one so quickly. The attorney said no problem, and he would make up the difference on the cost of the ticket so everyone could get back to the United States. Despite our manager's larcenous predilections—let's just call them misjudgments instead of criminal activities—Eric's attorney got Joe out of jail, paid the fine for Joe, reimbursed the stores for the bad checks, paid the postal bill because Joe tried to send the trunks of clothing with bad checks, and then was going to pay the difference on the cost of the tickets. I called Eric Burdon to thank him, and he said to me, "I'm going to take you guys out to dinner, and then I'll collect you in the morning."

All seemed copacetic with everyone, that is, everyone except me. I had been sexually taken advantage of the night before, and I was hurt, ashamed, angry, depressed, and overwhelmed. I couldn't eat or sit still. Worse, I didn't want to talk to anyone about it, not even my sister. So when night rolled around, I told everyone I would take the couch that night. When left alone, I snuck into the kitchen and grabbed a kitchen knife. I was brought up right, I thought of myself as a good person, I believed in God, but I said to myself, if he comes for me tonight, I'm going to kill him. I could not let him touch me again. I believe Barbara and Joan were smart enough to know my countenance, and they probably—although I never asked—strongly conveyed to Joe Jones that he needed to leave me alone. He didn't come, and I didn't sleep a wink. In the morning Barbara looked at me and asked, "Didn't you get any sleep?" I had put the kitchen knife away by that time and simply said, "I just did not feel like sleeping."

Eric came for us the next morning and Barbara told him, "When we get back to the United States and have time to go to the bank, get a certified check, we'll send it to you." Eric said, "No rush, sweetheart. When you can, send me the money." Joe didn't say anything, although he still had all our earnings in his pocket.

We finally got home and settled in. Later that evening Joe came down and Barbara asked, "Did you go to the bank and put the money in the account?" Joe said yes and that all was good. We all felt relieved, because we wanted to settle our debt with Eric and his attorney. Barbara asked Joe, "OK, great, and when are you going to write the check for Eric's lawyer?"

"Who?" Joe spat the word vehemently.

"Eric Burdon's lawyer," Barbara continued. "You know, the man who got you out of jail."

"I ain't paying him nothing," Joe smirked.

This wasn't what we wanted to hear. We were now standing in an earthquake. "Joe," Barbara said, "you can't mean this. This man saved you, saved us."

Joe laughed. "Well, that's something he had to pay me back for, because you know how the white people are. They are always using us and misusing us, and screwing our women."

The last comment was as if that kitchen knife from Eric's apartment went right through my chest. I got up from the table, went into the bedroom, and locked the door.

Barbara and Joan got into the argument with Joe, trying to point out the benevolence of Eric's actions, saying he didn't have to open his house for us to stay there, that the whole time we were there, he stayed at the Hilton. He didn't have to do that. And for this man to pay all the bills. Barbara had copies and she waved them at him.

"Fuck 'em, I ain't paying them back. End of argument."

We, of course, had no money to make good, and Joe's scheme worked.... All those purchases in England, and he didn't pay one dime out of his own pocket. My plan didn't come to fruition, as I left England without putting a knife through his neck. I should have, because things only got worse for me—I became Joe's victim.

We had only one bedroom. Barbara and Joan slept in the double bed in the bedroom, and I had the pull-out bed to myself in the living room. The configuration didn't bother us, because we figured we would start out with this one-bedroom apartment and then talk to the manager about a two-bedroom. At some point Joe had shelves put into our dining room and made it his office, telling us when we were on the road that he was going to use our place. So he changed the locks, keeping a key for himself. That meant he could get in and out of the apartment any time he wanted. He wouldn't even ring the bell, just walk in.

He knew I slept in the living room, and one night soon after our European trip, he came into the apartment. Everyone was asleep, but I woke up. When he came to the pull-out bed, he whispered, "I know you're not sleeping," and proceeded to take off his clothes. I tried to keep pretending I was asleep, but before I knew it, he was on top of me. I bit him on the lip. He stopped for a moment and said, "Now, why did you do that? What am I going to tell Marion?" I said, "Go upstairs and tell her whatever you want." He didn't stop until he was finished.

This went from one night to two nights to three nights to whenever we were home and he felt like doing it. If I complained or fought back, he would say to me, "I'm going to send you back to New Orleans on a Greyhound bus." He said he would then call my mother and tell her that I had been with the men in the band and they all said they had had me. He would tell my mother that after the tour, all the guys bragged I had been with all of them. I was a teenager, but emotionally and experientially I had not yet grown up. He had guardianship over me, and I believed him that he would call my mother. I believed he had the power to send me back to New Orleans. He knew he could do whatever he wanted to me.

At some point I couldn't bear it anymore, and I threw a heavy ashtray at him. He ducked and it didn't hit his body, but the defiant act shocked him. He called my mom and told her I was crazy. She said, "What do you mean, she is crazy? What are you talking about?" He said, "She threw an ashtray at me." She answered, "What did you do to her, because you probably deserved it?"

CHAPTER EIGHT

You Should Have Seen the Way He Looked at Me

The year 1964 ended with "You Should Have Seen the Way He Looked at Me" on the best-selling record charts, and a few months into 1965, "Iko Iko" did the same. The Dixie Cups continued to be in demand. We returned to top-notch venues such as the Apollo. A '65 flyer of the Dixie Cups in action noted, "Back at the Apollo by Popular Demand." We also performed at smaller locations such as The Castaways in North Carolina. That flyer reads: "Homecoming Week At Collegiate Carolina's Number I Club, The Castaways, 813 Dickinson Avenue, Fri. Nov. 5, The Dixie Cups, also Little David and The Wanderers, $4.00 per couple."

We were so singularly focused on being the Dixie Cups that the real world was passing us by and we barely paid attention. Civil rights, riots, Martin Luther King, President Johnson, the Vietnam War, and the Voting Rights Act were all big issues surrounding us, yet sliding behind the Dixie Cups like a backdrop on a stage. Still, as ingenuous as we were, you can't dissociate from real life, and eventually it all catches up to you. In the mid-1960s, it was a dangerous and changing world for Blacks, and in time it would encompass us as well.

Before I talk about the South, discrimination, and the Ku Klux Klan, I'll address the other overriding issue of the 1960s, the Vietnam War. In 1966 Joe had taken a trip down to the Dominican Republic, where he ended up hanging out with a group of men from the Department of Defense who were on vacation. Chatting them up, Joe boasted he was the manager of the Dixie Cups, the group that sang "Chapel of Love" and "Iko Iko." Defense Department officials were impressed and asked Joe if the Dixie Cups would like to come to Vietnam to entertain the troops. Of course, he said yes.

Truthfully, we weren't paying much attention to the Vietnam War, although there was one thing that caught our eyes and ears. During that year of '66, Muhammad Ali claimed he was a conscientious objector and was not going to fight in Vietnam. He famously said at the time, "I ain't got no quarrel with them Vietcong." Meanwhile, over in Southeast Asia, the war was heating up. In 1964 the United States had fewer than 24,000 soldiers in Vietnam. By 1966 that number vaulted to over 385,000. News stories about protests to the war started to become more frequent.

When we heard we would be going to Vietnam, we were excited. We knew there was a war going on, but heated debates and incidents between protestors and supporters of the war in the United States hadn't quite taken off yet, and the news then about the conflict was more low-key. It didn't seem to us to be such a big deal to go to Vietnam. We didn't perceive that we would be in harm's way. On the other hand, our mother was paying attention, and when we initially called to tell her we would be going, she went quiet on the telephone. For the Dixie Cups, the only problem was with Barbara, who hated shots, and when we were told we would have to take twenty-one inoculations, she almost bolted for her mommy in New Orleans. "Why so many?" she whined. As I liked to say, "Don't come to Barbara with a needle."

Most shows traveling to war zones were the Bob Hope–type extravaganzas with singers, movie stars, and curvaceous dancing girls. This wasn't a Bob Hope tour. It was just us, and it was bare bones. We didn't have a band. Joe played the piano, and he also had a record player and the records of our songs. Every place we went, Joe hooked it up. The troops didn't care. When we went out on stage, the guys screamed and hollered: "Can I have your autograph?" "Can I hold your hand?" "Can I touch you?" Those guys were really enthused that we were there.

It was only the Dixie Cups, and the tour would last about three months. It would have ended sooner, but Gen. William Westmoreland, the commander of US forces in Vietnam, asked us to stay longer to help celebrate the anniversary of one of the infantry battalions on the ground in the country. We had another scheduled gig for the US Air Force in Thule, Greenland, which we were supposed to do that December, but when the commanding general asks, you have to say, "Yes, sir!"

The trip was fun, interesting, exciting, eye-opening, and ultimately dangerous. We rode in helicopters, planes, and troop carriers from one end of the country to the other. The day we arrived, we were appointed an escort officer who ushered us to one of the big hotels in Saigon. I stepped out on the balcony to look around and knew I was no longer in a place even close to resembling the United States. From the start, it was a little weird, not because of the Vietnamese, but due to the American servicemen, both Black and white. When they saw us, they knew immediately we were Americans and would come over to us with tears in their eyes. When I asked our escort officer about these emotional demonstrations, he said some of these men had not seen an American woman, except maybe a nurse, in over six months, and just seeing us made them all a bit homesick. Sometimes a military man would approach me and ask, "Are you really an American woman?" At first we thought it was funny. Then we felt bad because these guys were in a war zone with their lives on the line and so emotionally fragile.

When we visited the men on remote bases outside of Saigon, we were warned of the dangers and told numerous words of caution. The one that I remember is "If you hear a hiss, then a boom, that means a bomb has already hit; if you hear a boom and then a hiss, that means a bomb has been sent out." To keep us from getting malaria, we also had to take these gigantic pills, which we could get down only cutting in half.

One time we were put aboard a Lockheed C-130 Hercules heading to an airbase in another part of Vietnam. There weren't any extravagant, protective troops with us, just our escort officer. As always, the other girls and I crowded the window seats to see the landscape below. We were coming in later than expected, and below we heard the booms and the gunfire. The plane passed over the base, and when we looked down, we could see a big hole in what looked like a stage. When I asked the escort about that, he sighed and said we weren't supposed to see that. What had happened was, at the time we were supposed to be on that stage, the Viet Cong, who had ascertained information that entertainers would be visiting the base at a particular time, launched rockets and mortars, one of which hit the target. From what we understood, there could have been a thousand troops, men and women, there to see us perform, and they would have been under fire as well. We were told not to land.

The men were so kind to us, often letting us pose with weapons standing before attack helicopters or on transports. When we left, they awarded us a certificate. For example, one award read: "The First Cavalry Division (Airmobile), The First Team, Honorary Sky Trooper Certificate is presented to Rosa Hawkins [Barbara and Joan got the same certificate], signed John Norton, Major General, United States Army, 1st Cavalry Division (Airmobile), Commanding."

The most cherished certificate came from General Westmoreland. That certificate reads: "Department of Defense, United States Military Assistance Command Vietnam, Certificate of Appreciation is awarded to Rosa Hawkins

[Barbara and Joan received the same certificate], For your outstanding contribution to the morale and welfare of the United States Armed Forces in the Republic of Vietnam by touring the command entertaining personnel of all branches of the military service, Saigon, Vietnam, 1 October 1966, signed W.C. Westmoreland, General, United States Army, Commanding."

From 1964 through the early 1970s, the Dixie Cups probably worked every military base in the United States. In August 1971, the *NCO Club News* noted: "The Dixie Cups, SOUL FAME DEBUTS THE DOVER AFB NCO CLUB THIS MONTH, The famous Dixie Cups, popular in the now soul world of entertainment have swung by on tour to put on a fantastic show 'soully' for you."

Less than a year later, in April 1972, the *NCO Club News* reported that we were back: "SOUL FAMOUS, The fabulous Dixie Cups are returning for a repeat performance right here on your NCO Club stage."

Ron Peters, a promoter based in Fayetteville, North Carolina, brought us back to Southeast Asia, a few years later, but this time to Thailand. We visited the military in other far lands as well. We adored Ron, a white southerner, but his location in the middle of North Carolina turned out to be the real danger for the Dixie Cups. In the mid-1960s, the American South could be just as precarious for "Negroes" as Vietnam was for American soldiers.

One always had to be careful on tours in the South. Dick Clark was cautious and protective, since his shows were always a mixed-race group of young performers. Many places in the South were segregated, and when we stopped for meals, Dick would get out of the bus, inquire if we all could eat at the restaurant, and if not he would find another restaurant that would accommodate us.

In the spring of 1965, the year the Voting Rights Act, which prohibited racial discrimination in elections, was passed, the Dixie Cups were booked on a long tour that would feature Gerry & the Pacemakers. This wasn't a Dick Clark Caravan of Stars tour, but an ABC-TV *Shindig* tour led by Jimmy O'Neill, who also hosted the television show. The tour was created by Selmur Productions, the producer of *Shindig!* The idea of the tour came about because other less scrupulous and fly-by-night tour companies were putting together packages of singers and calling their tours Shindig. In fact, Selmur Productions published an open letter saying, "It has come to our attention that a number of unauthorized, one-night stands, road shows and/or concerts utilizing the SHINDIG name ... have played various dates or are currently attempting to attain further bookings. Appropriate action will be taken with regard to these unauthorized uses."

By 1965 the post-Beatles invasion of British acts was swarming the American shores, and the competition for these performers was intense. Dick Clark's Caravan of Stars headlined Peter and Gordon, and Tom Jones. ABC-TV's *Shindig!* grabbed Gerry & the Pacemakers and the Australian band the Newbeats for limited runs on its tour. When the *Shindig* tour dipped into Virginia, the line-up was Gerry & the Pacemakers, Shirley Ellis, the Dixie Cups, Willie Nelson, Roosevelt Grier, Linda Gail, Jim Doval & the Gauchos, and Joey Paige.

We stopped to eat somewhere in Virginia, and Jimmy O'Neill went into the restaurant to find out if it could feed the tour. All of us in the bus got restless and walked out, just milling around. Just then a big theater not far away began to let out. As the crowd came toward all of us, just as a joke, we decided to sing the gospel/folk song, "We Shall Not be Moved," as if we were in that town for a civil rights protest. It was a juvenile and mischievous thing to do, because the police were called, and they came in force.

They said, "We know what you all are up to, now get on the bus."

Jimmie scrambled back and yelled at us like children, "Don't you know where you are?"

One policeman pulled Jimmie aside and barked, "You the boss of these children?" which made us laugh. So Jimmie explained we were all famous singers. The cops quickly changed their demeanor and now asked for autographs. Gerry Marsden, who was Gerry of Gerry & the Pacemakers, said, "I am not giving them my autograph." He didn't know the South. We did, and we didn't want the situation to turn brutal. Some of us on the bus hinted to Gerry that either he gives autographs, or the rest of us on the bus break his fingers. "Then I can't write," he pouted. The police came on the bus to gather autographs, including Gerry's.

The *Shindig* tour was greeted dismissively by many of the local newspapers. On April 22, 1965, the *Houston Post* review of the show dripped with condescension. Some choice comments from that review:

> Teenagers of formidable shriek-power nearly filled the hall and they produced a sound not unlike a jet engine's whine as a band on the stage struck up a pounding beat.
>
> Sue Thompson, a blonde in a blue sweater and skirt, came out as if she were running a kiddie show.... Sue Thompson came back and sang in a Donald Duck voice a sing [*sic*] about true confessions and a sweetheart named Norman.
>
> A little later Jim Douval [*sic*]and the Gauchos appeared. They turned out to be six youths with haircuts like New Guinea aborigines.
>
> [Then came our turn.] Six girls in orange outfits emerged to dance spasmodically in the popular Go-Go idiom and three other girls, later identified as The Dixie Cups appeared in glittering blue blouses and snug golden pants to sway on a pedestal at one side of the stage.... Then The Dixie Cups took center stage, two girls at one mike, one at the other. They executed rhythmic bumps as they sang. Sometimes they used tambourines.

From the critics there were only slings and arrows to cope with. We faced worse. Such as the time Ron Peters inadvertently booked us a job to entertain a local North Carolina branch of the Ku Klux Klan. When I think back on it, I remember Barbara mumbling, "If I get out of here, I'm going to beat Ron Peters until he turns black."

This is what happened. Ron received a call from a local businessman who told him his daughter was getting married and was a big fan of the song "Chapel of Love." The businessman heard that Ron represented the Dixie Cups and asked if he could book them for the wedding. Ron told him our price. The businessman said yes, and we were booked to entertain the wedding crowd at a special party for the daughter.

The arrangements were for them to pick us up at the airport, take us to the venue, where there would be a band to back us, and at the end of the day drive us back to the hotel. At the last minute, the transport couldn't make it, and Ron sent a young man to drive us. Ron would follow. So, we ended up heading down a deserted, two-lane road in the middle of nowhere when we noticed a paper sign tacked onto a wooden light pole. On the paper was an arrow pointing to the office of the Ku Klux Klan. I said to the driver, "Did you see that?" The driver answered, "Why do you think I'm sitting here so quietly ready to piss in my pants?" All I could think of was, "Lord, where is he sending us?"

There were no such things as cell phones back then. If you needed to call someone, you had to find a phone booth or a residence or business with a phone. We were nowhere. The driver asked, "What do you want me to do?" This was after Joan Marie had left the group and been replaced by singer Beverly Brown, who was getting very nervous. "Barbara," she exclaimed, "I'm not going on this gig. You better turn this car around."

Barbara looked at her watch, "We are so far into these woods, there is no point in turning around." She was right, because just up ahead were signs of civilization: six men, who on closer inspection were armed. They were waiting for us. The driver stopped the car, and one man approached. He looked in and said, "I guess you-all are the Dixie Cups."

Nobody wanted to answer, because we were too scared. He continued, "We're here to show you where to go. Just follow me in the green pickup truck."

I'm thinking, "The man got a green truck! This is not good." Armed white men in pickup trucks had a bad connotation: pictures of Black men being lynched in the South often included hooded men in an old pickup truck.

They led our car to this little hole-in-the-wall place where the party was to be held. "This is where you're going to be playing," we were told. "The band will be here within the hour, so just come on in and relax."

I'm thinking, "Are you out of your mind? I can't relax here." But he showed us to the dressing room. Of course there was no lock on the dressing room door.

We sat and waited for the band. When they arrived, it was time to get dressed. Beverly, looking at the door with no lock, protested, "I ain't taking my clothes off. They got no locks on the door."

"Please cooperate," Barbara pleaded.

"Why can't we go on with what we have on?" said the very frightened Beverly.

"Because that's not us," Barbara, ever the professional, responded. "We don't go on the road with blue jeans and T-shirts and then go on the stage in those same clothes." Ron Peters and his associate had arrived by this time, and we had them stand outside the door. When we had finished dressing, we signaled we were ready, and Ron and his associate came in.

"Ron Peters," I said, "I hope you said goodbye to your wife and child tonight, because if we get out of here, we are going to kill you."

"Do you think I booked you out here knowing what it was?" he said. "The man did not have a drawl, he was very pleasant on the phone and sounded intelligent. He just told me he wanted to hire the Dixie Cups."

The daughter came into the dressing room, looked at Ron, and said you-all gotta come and dance with me. We all looked at Ron, who appeared as if he himself was being led to an execution. He said, "If this man wants me to dance with his daughter, well, I'm going to dance with his daughter." Later, after our performance, they brought us food, but we didn't know if we should eat it or not. It was an unusual experience.

It didn't always go that way in the South. As a Black person, you never felt secure, because danger could come at you from anywhere.

We were playing a military base in central North Carolina with two drivers Ron hired. They were driving a Volkswagen Beetle, so the three of us, Barbara, Beverly Brown, and I, were crowded in the backseat. That was OK, as we were headed back to Fayetteville, which wasn't a long ride. It was a good show, and now it was later in the evening and we were hungry. We weren't on an interstate, just a main road with a truck stop, and that's where we pulled in to get a bite to eat. The five of us walked into the restaurant, which was crowded with mostly young white men—not a good sign in the South in the 1960s. Beverly muttered, "Lord, I don't feel good about this. We need to go straight back to Ron Peters's house, and I'm sure his wife will feed us something." Barbara was again the voice of reassurance and said, "It's going to be all right." Beverly shook her head, "I'm not feeling this."

Meanwhile, the N-word was being slung loudly across the room. I had never heard that word used so often in one place in my whole life. We sat down at a table, and the waitress came over and dropped off menus and took an order for coffees. The driver and his friend, looking around, whispered that we needed to get out of there. Beverly, who was a smoker, took out three cigarettes and told me, "Here, take this." I didn't smoke and told her I didn't want a cigarette. "This will help us get out of here," Beverly said, "because if they come to do anything, go for the eyes with the cigarette." I took that cigarette, and so did Barbara.

The N-word was getting louder and more threatening. The waitress came back and said, "I'm so sorry these guys are being assholes. But don't worry about them, Mr. Brown got his eye on them. What do you all want to eat?"

I said, "We were hungry before. Now we're not so sure."

"I know all them boys," said the waitress. "They are just bigmouths."

I looked around to see where to go if we had to make a break for it. The place had two doors, one at one end of the dining room and the second at the other end where the cash register was. The driver looked nervously to his friend and said, "Go ahead and bring them to the car. I'll pay the bill."

I was still thinking as I got up, These aren't evil people, although everything about our situation was screaming danger. Peril was slapping us right in the face. The driver went to the register to pay the bill.

"Mr. Brown says this one is on him," he was told.

"Thank you, ma'am, but we need to pay the bill," the driver answered politely, so the waitress took the money.

The other guy walked us to the car, and we got in. He walked back to the restaurant, which was a big mistake. A group of white guys, armed with guns and chains, backed him up against a plate glass window. Oh my God, they are going to kill him, I thought.

The man referred to as Mr. Brown rushed out.

"Why did you let those N-words in the restaurant? This is our place," said one of the boys. "You let them in our place."

"This isn't 'our place,'" Mr. Brown said. "This is my place. And these young ladies are the singing group the Dixie Cups. You know that song 'Chapel of Love'?"

"What you mean, these N-words sang that song?"

"Don't call them that. They are nice ladies, and they just got finished working at the military base."

Another boy yelled, "I don't care who they are, they are just N-words."

Mr. Brown turned out to be a number one man. Before he came outside, he'd called the state troopers, and just then we heard sirens, and tires hitting the gravel. Four or five trooper cars came screaming forward.

"What? You called the troopers on us?" yelled someone in the group of boys.

We pushed out of the car only to hear a rifle being cocked. "Let him go, boys."

Our hearts were beating so fast, we probably could have sung "Iko Iko" and done a dance to it, that's how scared we were.

A trooper said to us, "You all need to get back in the car," and then, when we had, he asked, "Where you headed?"

"Fayetteville!" we yelled back.

With everyone back in the car, the head trooper leaned in the window. "I'm sending one car in front and one behind. Each car will have three officers with guns loaded."

We gave the trooper our agent's address and phone number. "I will have him waiting for you," said the trooper.

When the three vehicles pulled up to Ron's house, the local police were already there. Ron fired the two guys. We protested, pleading not to fire them, and that they did the best they could under stressful circumstances.

"You're not from this state, you're from Louisiana," he said. "They are from this state and knew the chance they were taking in stopping at that truck stop. They should have brought you here, and we would have fixed you something. How do you think I would have felt if I would have to call your mothers and tell them something terrible happened to you?"

We were exhausted and told Ron we just wanted to go back to the hotel and go to bed.

"You're not going to the hotel," he continued. "We checked you guys out of there. You're staying here. The police will be outside until you leave this city."

We had three more nights with Ron.

Despite all those strange conditions on the road, under threats from the Viet Cong or the Ku Klux Klan or just racist young white men, perhaps the greatest indignity inflicted on the Dixie Cups came not from outside agitation and threats but from within our inner circle. Indeed, it was such a low blow to Barbara and me that we finally realized it was time to leave Joe Jones and even New York behind. It was time to go home. The dream had faded.

The Dixie Cups from the start were Barbara, Joan Marie Johnson, and me. Then Joan had to leave us.

The first woman to replace Joan was Beverly Brown. Joe heard her in a New Orleans club and brought her up to New York. Charles Brimmer, a New Orleans singer, who at some point worked with Wardell Quezergue, David Batiste, and David Bartholomew, for a short time had his own label, Brimmer Records, and one of acts he recorded was Beverly Brown singing "Don't Break My Heart." We got along fine with her, but Joe started using her physically. She also never saw any money. She went on gigs with us and had to ask Barbara for cash. It wasn't as if we had free money to spare, so Barbara said she had to ask Joe, who told her you're not getting any money until you do this or this.

Terrible for Beverly, but it was a release for me. When she got tired of being taken advantage of sexually, she called her parents and told them she wanted to come home. Unfortunately for her, like other women who thought Joe was the world and got with him, she found out he was all empty promises. In the end, she just couldn't take him anymore. Like Joan Marie, Beverly also had health issues. She was a lot of fun, and when Barbara and I moved back to New Orleans, we got back together with her. She became the Dixie Cups' third singer into the 1980s.

Another of the people Joe Jones recruited and signed to be the third Dixie Cup was a singer named Eleanore Mills. I don't know where Joe found her, but he put Eleanore under contract, and she went on her first road trip to the South as a member of the Dixie Cups.

We were on a swing through Georgia, first appearing in Columbus, and Joe began promoting her to the local press. On May 18, 1968, the *Ledger* in Columbus published a news story with the headline "Dixie Cups Appear Here," but above that were the names: Rosa, Eleanore, Barbara. The columnist, Nell Fowler, began with this introduction: "Since the Dixie Cups out-sold the Beatles in 1965, they have been touring every state in the union except Alabama, and they've been mobbed in England and cheered wildly in Vietnam."(In 1965 the Dixie Cups album outsold the Beatles album, and the Dixie Cups received the annual GeeGee Award from *16* magazine.)

Barbara and Joe did the interview with Nell, and the promotion of Eleanore by Joe got slipped into the discussion:

> Two of the girls, Rosa and Barbara Hawkins, are sisters from New Orleans. The third is Eleanore Mills of New York, who will soon cut her first single, "Telephone Booth." The regular third member of the group, Joan Johnson, is sick and couldn't make this trip. She, too, is from New Orleans, where the group was first discovered by [Joe] Jones, who took them to New York to groom them. Their first recording was "Chapel of Love," and as Barbara, the spokesman for the girls, says, it went "Boom."

Joe was the pianist on this tour, for which he got paid extra from the Dixie Cups, but the money wasn't the issue with Joe this time. Besides getting next to Eleanore, he had a grander plan—he wanted to be the next Berry Gordy of Motown. The big news in the "soul" music world at the end of the 1960s was that Mr. Gordy was going to break up the most successful girl group trio ever, the Supremes, and make Diana Ross a solo act. He had already moved in that direction by changing the name of the group from just the Supremes to Diana Ross & the Supremes.

Joe's sly idea that he never discussed with us was to put Eleanore up front as the lead singer of the Dixie Cups and introduce the act as Eleanore and the Dixie Cups. While it took us by surprise on the night of the Atlanta show, we reacted immediately. When we walked on stage, Barbara gave a side glance that said to me, "I don't think so."

We did the show, and Barbara took the lead from Eleanore, who had no recourse but to step back. I wouldn't let her stand next to me. She had to stand behind me and do background singing.

While Joe's experiment failed, one of his endearing traits was vengefulness, and we expected some kind of retribution.

The next morning before it was time to leave, Joe made sure to collect our pay from the owner of the club. Then he rang our room and told us to bring our luggage down while he checked us out of the hotel. When we got to the lobby, he was at the front desk and told us, "Eleanore is in the car, and she'll open it for you."

We brought the luggage to the car and knocked on the window. Eleanore, sitting in the passenger seat, wouldn't turn her head to see who it was, but of course she knew we were there. We knocked again and signaled to her to lower the window. She wouldn't turn in our direction. I said, "Eleanore, what's going on? Open the trunk so we can put our suitcases in." She didn't say anything. When she saw Joe approaching the car, she unlocked his door. He jumped in the car and prepared to drive off. Barbara and I were still standing on the sidewalk with our luggage.

Barbara yelled to him, "What are you doing?"

Joe stopped the car and rolled down the driver's-side window. He yelled to us, "Find your own way to New York or New Orleans the best way you can." And just like that, he and Eleanore drove off, leaving us there alone on the street.

Joe didn't know that we had friends in that city. So after being stranded, I called my girlfriend from high school, who was excited to hear from us. We asked if we could come and sit down and talk. My friend was a stewardess, as were all her roommates. At her apartment she asked if we had money to get back to New York, and I had to admit we didn't, because Joe, our manager, had it all with him. She and her two roommates got money together for Barbara, and the next morning they brought us to the airport, where we bought a ticket. They even gave us money to get a taxi from the airport to Manhattan. When the taxi pulled up, Joe happened to be coming out of the apartment building, and he stood there and looked at us with his mouth hanging open. We passed him without saying a word.

Sam, the doorman, said, "Welcome home," and then whispered, "You all need to get rid of the piece of shit." We went upstairs. We were tired, and we were tired of Joe.

He came down about three that morning because he had keys to our apartment. I came out of the bedroom and said this was not going to work. I told him, "You need to get out of here right now on your own, or I'm calling the police." He said they couldn't do anything. I said, "This apartment is in our name, not yours. Because you have keys, that doesn't mean a damn thing. Now you have a choice. You either turn around and walk out, or I'm going to call the police." He said, "We'll see about this," and walked out.

The next day we told him and Marion to take the piano out of the apartment, and the shelves he had installed. Marion asked, how are we going to do that? My response was, "You can carry it on your back as far as I care; we just want it out by tonight." About three in the morning, I heard this squeaking in the apartment. I opened the bedroom door and looked out. Joe and Marion were rolling the piano out of the apartment and out the door.

What happened to Eleanore?

One day soon afterward, she, along with her three brothers, came to the building and rang our doorbell. Eleanore asked if they could come up. We said, "For what? We really don't have anything to say to you." She answered, "I really need to apologize." So we let her in, and she came up with her brothers. Eleanore asked, "Can you call Joe and have him come down here?" Barbara and I still weren't feeling very obliging to her. I said, "You call him. The phone is right there." She dialed and talked with him briefly. Joe came down and met her three brothers, who told him in no uncertain terms he was never even to talk to or approach their sister ever again. One said to him, "If you see her on the street, you best cross over, because if you don't, they will be picking you up with the trash. Now, you go upstairs and get her contract." Joe had seen this scene before. He went upstairs with two of the brothers at his side. They took the contract from him, and Eleanore disappeared from Joe's life and ours. She had a nice voice, but he had no intention to record her. He just wanted to sleep with her.

In 1974 Eleanore recorded an album called *This Is Eleanore Mills*. She continued to release singles and EPs through the 1980s and into the 1990s.

The Atlanta incident was the last straw, or the cherry on top of the cake, depending on how you look at it. Barbara and I decided to continue our career but without Joe. The trouble was, other agents were not going to touch us as long as there existed an association with Joe Jones. When we said we weren't with him anymore and they checked it out, Joe would say if they booked the Dixie Cups, he was going to throw an injunction at them. That's when Barbara and I opted to find jobs outside the music industry, thinking if we could just hold on long enough, Joe would be out of the picture. It was at the beginning of winter 1968 that Joe figured out we were working and came to our apartment asking for money.

We left New York, because I got upset with Barbara. She is such a goodhearted person. She can't turn anyone down, and when he found out we were working, he told us his sob story. Later, in our apartment, I reiterated: "Don't give him any money. We worked hard for this, and even so we can barely pay our own rent." Barbara said, "Yeah, I know, but because he has those three kids, and it's getting colder." She gave him the money for the rent and to buy food, so I got mad and said, "We are going home."

We sold all our furniture to a girlfriend who was moving to the big city. By early winter 1969, the Dixie Cups had returned to New Orleans.

CHAPTER NINE

Iko Iko

To the Dixie Cups, "Iko Iko" was a simple song, a very simple song, but over the years so many different people wanted a part of it that it became more complicated just by its existence. Since the record's release in 1965, other musicians, ethnologists, linguists, unscrupulous managers, and, more recently, beneficiaries have tried to take and take apart the song, so I have given the song its own chapter and will try to touch on all its different aspects, its meaning, and even its origin.

The Dixie Cups and band were recording the songs for our first Red Bird album, called *Chapel of Love*, the same as our hit single. This was before albums became an art form. Albums were just another part of the promotion scheme for pop singers at the time, and record companies basically wanted to get these done as quickly and as cheaply as possible. The way that was done was to blitz through as many songs as possible in one long recording session. Joe decided to skip this long day, and he instead went back to New Orleans.

We entered the Mirasound Recording Studio in New York in the morning, and by evening we were still there. Everyone was beat, so Jerry said to all, "Let's take a two-hour break, then come back and finish." Jeff and Ellie had left already. They probably weren't even in the building. Most of the band and anyone else in the studio still around couldn't wait to get out of there, and they would all be gone those two hours even if they were just heading for dinner and drinks.

We, the Dixie Cups, were still in the studio after everyone left. Jerry, who was with the engineer, came in and asked if we wanted to go out for dinner. After talking amongst ourselves, we said we would just order something from somewhere nearby and eat in the studio. We were also a bit weary and didn't feel like going into the crowded Manhattan streets to look for a restaurant. And that's what we did. We ordered food and then sat around the studio waiting for it to be delivered. We thought Jerry and the engineer had left, but they hadn't. They were back in the control booth. We just didn't know it.

While waiting, and out of boredom, we started bouncing around "Iko Iko," which was a New Orleans "hymn" we used to hear our grandma sing all the time. (Technically, the tune was more of a chant, but Barbara and I were born and raised in New Orleans, and we always referred to our grandmother's song as a hymn. Hereafter I will use the word "chant.") We heard it so often we pretty much remembered most of the song. This was a fun thing for us to do, because we accompanied our version of "Iko Iko" with a lot of percussion. One of us was beating on a metal ashtray, one of us was smacking an aluminum chair, and one of us was tapping on a Coke bottle. After going on for a few minutes, we heard Jerry's voice through the loudspeakers. "Hey, can you do that again?"

Well, that was a surprise. We didn't know anyone was still in the studio. We signaled sure, why not. And we did it one more time. Jerry just let us run with whatever we had in the tank. That was it. There were never any more takes.

In all the stories about the recording of "Iko Iko," someone always brings up what we at the time called the calypso box, but what others refer to as the Jamaica box. It was, I learned later, a souvenir Jeff and Ellie brought back from their honeymoon in Jamaica. Basically, it was a wooden box with a hole in the front and four prongs. The musician would sit on the box to play. Sometimes it's called a marimbula, and it was used often when Jamaican musicians played mento, a precursor to reggae. Mike Stoller came into the studio and added the calypso box sound. If you listen closely, you can hear this bong, bong, bong sound, which is the echo-y box. That is the only other instrument added to the original "Iko Iko" recording.

I had read somewhere that Jeff or Ellie asked us to sing this line or that, which is all untrue. First of all, they weren't there at the recording. Afterward, they wouldn't know what to add, because what we were singing about was something cultural that happens in New Orleans. They were New Yorkers and knew nothing about Cajun, Creoles, or the backdrop to Mardi Gras.

Jerry asked us who wrote the song, and we said, "We did." We signed writers' papers to that effect, and Jerry quickly sent it all off for the song to be registered in our names. This was done so rapidly because Jerry and Mike didn't want to have a problem with Joe. They didn't say that to us, but we figured it out for ourselves.

The other odd thing was that no one ever asked us to write down the words. Someone at Red Bird or elsewhere just took it off the recording. If you listen to the original recordings, those are all the original words we sang, except for the line "I'm gonna set your flag on fire." We originally sang "gonna set your ass on fire." Red Bird told us we could not say that on the record. That was the only change.

"Iko Iko" lyrics:

> Talk-in' 'bout, Hey now ! Hey now ! I-ko, I-ko, un-day
> Jock-a-mo fee-no ai na-né, jock-a-mo fee na-né
> Look at my king all dressed in red I-ko, I-ko, un-day.
> I bet-cha five dol-lars he'll kill you dead, jock-a-mo fee na-né.

This is a Mardi Gras song, and back when we were young, different neighborhood groups competing in the Mardi Gras parade would organize as "Indian tribes." These tribes mainly consisted of African Americans who, since the mid-1800s, dressed up for Mardi Gras wearing costumes reflective of Native Americans. The phrase "my king" refers to the head of the tribe or the chief. A flag boy was someone who would signal when the next tribe would be parading down the street.

One year Barbara had been a full participant in these Mardi Gras activities as the queen of the Wild Magnolia tribe. The chief spotted Barbara, just asked her to be queen, and she said yes. Barbara came home and looked for me to see if I wanted to go as well. I told her, "I'm not walking from one end of New Orleans to the other."

Every part of New Orleans has an Indian tribe, and they all mass at Mardi Gras. The Indians take a year to make their costumes. The purpose of the tribes is to look wonderful, walk the streets, compete with other tribes for the best look, bring happiness, and gain recognition.

As a queen, Barbara danced and walked behind the chief throughout the parade. She also got to wear an Indian costume not unlike the ones the Dixie Cups wore for the "Iko Iko" photo shoot, plus an apron decorated in front and back, vest and crown. Everyone puts a lot of work into creating their own beautiful costumes, from the cloth to the beads. It's all very competitive, as every tribe wants to look better than the others. The entourage doesn't give out things to the crowd; the crowd gives small items to the entourage. "Our job," said Barbara, "was have our picture taken, dance, and make people happy." She also helped someone across the street, a difficulty in the middle of a parade.

That year I watched Mardi Gras on the television, and I saw her. Barbara was having a ball.

Red Bird liked our three-part-harmony sound so much that those were the songs the company pushed first—"Chapel of Love," "People Say," etc. "Iko Iko" was so different that I really can't say if it was ever on Jeff and Ellie's or Jerry and Mike's radar at all. The album came out. Jerry and Mike had a publisher in Europe they worked with, and somehow the music publisher got "Iko Iko" to a local deejay, who was really enthused about the song and played it often. In fact, he called us from Europe to let us know he had been playing it all night and kids were jamming the lines asking for the song. We were confused and asked, "What do you mean you've been playing it," because it was nowhere to be heard in the United States. He said he got a copy of it from Red Bird, and it was burning up the airwaves. That forced Red Bird to release the song back at home, which didn't happen until 1965.

When we toured England in April 1965, we appeared on the *Shivaree* television show, where we sang "Iko Iko" and "Chapel of Love." Also on that show were other American acts: Major Lance, Freddy Cannon, and the Hondells. Three months later we were back on the show, but by this time we were recording with ABC/Paramount, so we sang our other Mardi Gras–based tune, "Two-Way-Poc-A-Way," along with "I'm Gonna Get You Yet." Other guests included the Rolling Stones.

In May 1965 "Iko Iko" reached #20 on the record charts—not bad considering what was happening in the music world. Starting on April 10, the British groups were so popular they dominated the #1 slot on the US *Cashbox* lists. First came Freddie and the Dreamers ("I'm Telling You Now") for two weeks, then Wayne Fontana and the Mindbenders ("The Game of Love") for one week, then Herman's Hermits ("Mrs. Brown You've Got a Lovely Daughter") for three weeks, then the Beatles ("Ticket to Ride") for a week. It took the Beach Boys' "Help Me, Rhonda" to knock the Brits out of the top slot. Except for the Supremes and other Motown songstresses, the girl group sound was toast. "Iko Iko" thankfully was something different, which was why it did so well.

Red Bird, trying to cash in on the success of the song as quickly and cheaply as possible, reissued the *Chapel of Love* album from the year before but now called it the *Iko Iko* album. The songs on the B-side ran in the same order as on the *Chapel of Love* album, except "Iko Iko" was taken out and put on the A-side, and "Another Boy Like Mine" was moved from the A-side to the B-side. The A-side order was remixed, with "Iko Iko" the first song instead of "Chapel of Love." Since this was a straight, albeit disguised, reissue, songs such as "Little Bell" and "You Should Have Seen the Way He Looked at Me" were not on the album. Although both records charted as singles, neither was meant to be on an album.

There was one major improvement in the reissue. A great black-and-white photo of the Dixie Cups dominated the cover, from left to right, Barbara, Joan Marie, and me leaning in because I was so much taller than the other girls. Above the photo, the title ran like this: the words "*IKO IKO*" in capital letters at the top and underneath "THE DIXIE CUPS" also in capital letters.

For the Dixie Cups, this success brought us immediate problems. (As they say in the music business, "Whenever there is a hit, there's a writ.") When Joe came back in town, he asked how the recording session went. We told him it all went fine and, oh, by the way, we recorded "Iko Iko."

Boom! He exploded like a tossed hand grenade. He called us all kinds of names from A to Z, and then from AA to ZZ. He told us how stupid we were and how the white man was going to use us. We sat there in our apartment looking like three little scared cats—we had no idea what he was talking about. Then we said no one was going to take advantage of us, because we signed the copyright papers. He stopped. "What do you mean, you signed papers?" I said, "That we wrote the song." He started in again and flew out of the apartment. He went straight to Mike and Jerry to get them to void the papers. He wanted to put the lie out that he had something to do with writing the song. He was trying to make Jerry and Mike believe that song was written at his house in New Orleans with his wife and secretary (mistress). He sent Jerry and Mike a new writer's contract in which he included his whole family and his mistress's whole family as cowriters. Mike and Jerry didn't bite, and Joe figured he would get even by taking us to another record label.

The record was a hit, and not long after, we were contacted by the lawyers for James "Sugar Boy" Crawford, a New Orleans rhythm and blues singer we'd never heard of. It turns out Crawford had a local record called "Jock-A-Mo" that sold well in New Orleans during the Mardi Gras season of 1954. Not only had we not heard of Crawford, we had no idea he recorded a song using the same New Orleans Mardi Gras chant our grandmother sang. It was kind of a call-and-response, almost a victory call of one Mardi Gras Indian tribe over another.

As Crawford himself told Jeff Hannusch, author of *I Hear You Knockin': The Sound of New Orleans Rhythm and Blues*, "'Jock-A-Mo' came from two songs that I used to hear the Indians sing. I put that together with other musicians. We used to see the Indians a lot because we lived near the Battlefield [Claiborne and Poydras Streets]."

Crawford claimed he was the songwriter for "Iko Iko," but in reality he had just tapped into the same existing well of inspiration and existing New Orleans music heritage that we did. If you pull up the two songs on the internet, you hear two different treatments of the same base of Creole/Native American wording. Crawford uses a standard Caribbean/calypso rhythm, circa 1950s.

There's a rhythm and blues horn break in the middle, and finally he takes a male interpretation, that is, the line "Look at my queen all dressed in red / I'll bet you five dollars she'll kill you dead." When the Dixie Cups sang "Iko Iko," it was more percussive, because we were doing nothing but banging on existing items in the studio. Again, that's the only instrumentation besides the Jamaica box added afterward. Finally, the wording is female slanted. The line "See that guy all dressed in green / Iko, Iko un-day / He's not a man, he's a lovin' machine," is all Dixie Cups.

Needless to say, there was a lot of noise at the judicial hearing about ownership rights to the song, and the judge got aggravated about the repetitive arguments from Crawford, us, and even Joe. The judge didn't think the words were the same and said something to the effect of "I cannot sit here and say, Mr. Crawford, that this is your song, because to me it sounds like another song even though some of it is similar." In the end, the judge split the ownership rights, giving 60 percent to the Dixie Cups and 40 percent to James "Sugar Boy" Crawford. Unfortunately, life didn't get easier for Crawford. I heard that his manager never paid him his due. I'm not saying Crawford wasn't talented or deserving, but we had never heard of him, or his song, and our creation of "Iko Iko" had nothing to do with him.

When there's money involved, these issues don't ever end. A few years back, Crawford's grandson tried to get the Dixie Cups to give up our rights to the song. That wasn't going to happen.

I have a 1965 news clipping from a forgotten newspaper, which I kept because it early on addressed the lyrics of "Iko Iko" and other misinformation. The journalist was Ronnie Oberman, who wrote:

> Only The Dixie Cups know for sure. At least, that's what the people around the offices of Red Bird Records say about the popular threesome's latest single "Iko Iko." No one at Red Bird seems to know exactly how "Iko Iko" came about, except that the song was derived from a Creole tune popular in New Orleans. "The Dixie Cups wrote it," says Bonnie Leon of Red Bird. "Their home is in New Orleans, where they got the idea." Bonnie would not venture to guess the meaning of some of the tune's lines, let alone the significance of the title. . . . Bonnie says the tune originally was released last summer in The Dixie Cups' first album "Chapel of Love." It was included, she explains, "so that they could ask people what they thought about it." Response from around the country was great, Bonnie says, adding that Red Bird executives "liked the song all along. So they decided to release it as a single."

According to Bonnie, Red Bird's corporate spokesperson, the instrumentation included a metal can opener banging against a glass ashtray and a pencil striking the top of a recording studio piano. About the only thing she got right was the opening line, "Only The Dixie Cups know for sure."

As to the lyrics of "Iko Iko," it's doubtful if any popular song has been so linguistically researched. There is even a YouTube video explaining it all—which, by the way, says the song is entirely Louisiana Creole except for one phrase that is Native American. On the other hand, an *Offbeat* magazine article from 2009 has the lyrics originating in West Africa, where "ayeko, often repeated as ayeko, ayeko is a popular chant meaning well done or congratulations." Another researcher argues the song's roots are a combination of Yoruba (African) and Creole, and "Aiku, Aiku nde" means "God is watching." The YouTube video says "Iko Iko" was a misinterpretation of a Creole shout, "Akout, Akout," which means "listen up." That author maintains the line "Jock-a-mo fee-no ai na-né, jock-a-mo fee na-né" has the back part of the line as Creole and first part, "Jock-a-mo," as Native American, again a misinterpretation, this time of the word "Chockma," meaning "it's good."

"Iko Iko" has been such an adaptable, playful song that it's been used in countless movies and television shows and recorded by everyone from the Grateful Dead to the singer Sia. All that creates income, and if there is money involved, then Joe Jones is not going to be far away. Sure enough, Joe Jones and family filed a copyright registration in 1991 saying they wrote the song. Somehow he was able to illegally obtain the licensing rights to "Iko Iko" outside of North America, which he used to license the song to the movie *Mission Impossible 2*. We sued in the United States District Court for the Eastern District of Louisiana. The official title of the suit was *Rosa Lee Hawkins, Barbara Ann Hawkins, and Joan Marie Johnson (plaintiffs) versus Joe Jones dba Melder Publishing Co. (Defendant)*.

In the end it was a judicial landslide victory for the Dixie Cups. Every claim by Joe Jones was dismissed.

As to the large amount of money due to the Dixie Cups from the lawsuit, we have yet to see a penny of it.

For a song composed by the Dixie Cups in 1964, one would think all the legal battles are finally over. That would be incorrect. Joan Marie died in 2016 and left her rights to the song "Iko Iko" to her goddaughter. A year later that, too, ended in a legal battle. According to news accounts, Artist Rights Enforcement for more than a decade collected a 50 percent contingency fee under a contract with EMI's predecessor, after representing Joan Marie and protecting her royalty interest in the song. The goddaughter took the position that Artist Rights is not entitled to continue collecting the songwriter royalties after Joan Marie died.

This legal conflict has nothing to do with my sister and me.

CHAPTER TEN

Walking to New Orleans

The Dixie Cups sang the highly romantic ballad "Chapel of Love," but by choice neither Barbara nor I ever married. Only Joan Marie made it to the "Chapel of Love."

This doesn't mean we never fell in love, or didn't have boyfriends, or weren't asked by beaus to marry. It just meant we didn't cross the threshold. The reasons vary, but for me it was about commitments to my career; once I entered the music industry, that's where I wanted to be.

It's not that I gave up a lot, as I was a late bloomer going back to my years in high school. I didn't date through most of my teen years, never kissed a boy until I was seventeen, and didn't have a boyfriend until I was in twelfth grade. The big deal about having a boy your last year in school is that you'll have someone to take you to the prom. My boyfriend was a year older than me, graduated a year ahead, and by the end of my senior year was in the military. Thankfully, he did call me to say he was coming back to New Orleans to take me to my prom. Two of my best friends were also dating guys in the service, and the big chatter between us was about how our guys were coming home and would be taking us to the prom in their uniforms.

Even if one was closely following the news at the time, which I wasn't, it was possible to miss the fact that the Central Intelligence Agency sponsored a rebel group to land in Cuba and overthrow Fidel Castro. The event has come to be known as the Bay of Pigs invasion, and it happened on April 17, 1961. The rebel (mostly Cuban exiles) invasion was an embarrassing failure to the administration of President John F. Kennedy, and the immediate repercussion was a directive of readiness to certain branches of the military. My boyfriend had been in the service since the Bay of Pigs, and by the time of my prom he was still on active duty. He called to say his leave had been cancelled.

I was coming home from graduation rehearsal, and when my mother saw me she called, "Hurry up, Edward is on the phone."

When he said he wasn't going to be able to take me to the prom, I got angry at him because I was young and stupid. This was my selfish thinking: Why were commands in the military more important than my having a date for the prom? After all, I already had my gown. We discussed it and Edward asked his best friend, Harold, who had a younger brother named Morris, if Morris could step in and take me to the prom. Despite his being a year younger than me, I decided to let Morris take me to the prom. We would arrive by taxi. I know what you're thinking—a taxi? But in those days, when no one had a lot of money, arriving by taxi was the equivalent of arriving by limousine today. Back then you could tell it was prom night by all the taxis lining up to drop off teenagers. Morris was a nice guy. We did have fun, and that was it. The evening was never meant to be more than one evening out.

Tension with the Soviet Union over Cuba died down, and Edward eventually was granted leave to come back to New Orleans. I was still being ridiculous, exclaiming, "You don't like me, because if you did, you would have said your girlfriend is graduating and you had to come home." Of course, he tried to explain the way of the military and that no one was going on leave unless ill. My mother chimed in, "Don't talk to him like that, Rose. He couldn't help it. He's in the military, and he has to do what the military tells him to do."

That relationship ended because I was very immature. Soon afterward I entered Southern University. At the time, Joan Marie and Barbara were dating two brothers. There was a third, younger brother named Stephen, and everyone conspired to get us together—and we did become a couple. When I was at college, Stephen would come and pick me up. If it was raining, I would call him to give me a ride. When we started going together, we would go to this neighborhood bar and restaurant, but we had to enter through the restaurant door, because we couldn't get a beer as we were underage. Then I went to New York to record that first time. After a few weeks, we were back home again.

One night I got a call from Joan Marie, who was with her boyfriend, the older brother of Stephen, and with Stephen as well. "It's Friday night and I know you're not doing anything. And Stephen would like to see you."

I hemmed and hawed.

Joan Marie countered, "Don't tell me you don't like Stephen a lot."

"I do, but I don't want to see him right now. You know how I am."

"Yes I do, you are disgusting," she said with a laugh. "And he's standing right here."

"What?" I gasped. "He's standing right there?"

She answered, "Don't talk to me with your tongue between your teeth."

"Okay, what time are you coming to pick me up?"

We all went out to the movies, and my relationship with Stephen kicked back in. The brothers used to like to work on their cars, so Joan Marie, Barbara, and I would hang out at the garage and watch them tinker about. Their father was Creole. If Stephen and I were sitting on the porch, I would, out of courtesy, always address him: "Hi, Mr. X, how are you doing?" He would say something back that to my ear was incomprehensible. I would look over to Stephen and shrug: "What did your dad say?" Stephen laughed, "I don't know what he said. Maybe it was what are ya-all doing sitting on my porch?" He had such a deep drawl, and since he never opened his mouth when he talked, we used to call him the grumbler.

Stephen and I went out together often until "Chapel of Love" was released and the Dixie Cups were called back to New York. Stephen looked at me and said, "You're just going back to New York?" I remember saying something such as, "Yeah, I have a career [oh, wasn't I so grown-up!], and I need to go back to New York." Over the next few years, we would write or call, but it wasn't a serious thing. Still, all those years on the road with those handsome young singers, and I never once had an affair with any of them. Well, there was Joe Jones abusing me, so that might have had something to do with it.

When I returned to New Orleans in 1969, Stephen and I got back together. He asked me to marry him. I told him no. I wasn't ready to give up my career. We later had a son together. I figured I could balance being a mother and a singer, but I couldn't balance being a mother, a singer, and a wife.

I never had another serious boyfriend after that, partly because I wanted to put all my concentration on being a good mother, a Dixie Cup, and a better person.

Getting reestablished with Stephen proved a lot easier than getting the Dixie Cups back on tour—until Joan Marie straightened us out once and for all.

When we went back to New Orleans and settled back in with our mom, we started all over again. This time we were no longer rookies; we were veterans of the music industry, having been at it for the past five years. We knew the agencies that booked us in the past, plus we had quite a few other contacts scattered all over the country. Barbara and I worked as a back office team, writing letters, making contacts, calling people directly. We were asked if we had a promotional kit, which we did. Some asked what kind of shows we were doing now. A lot of friendly secretaries said they would be getting back to us, yet they never seemed to. The problem continued to be Joe Jones. There were those agencies that knew him and didn't want to work with him again. Although we were in New Orleans and he was in New York, it was suspected there was still a connection, even though we maintained we quit him. Joe didn't make it any easier, because he put out the word that if anyone hired us, he would sue the venue. Even if they didn't believe him, even if they wanted to hire us—and most people said they did—no one wanted a legal battle.

Joan Marie had at that point a regular day job. She so hated Joe, she didn't even want to be a Dixie Cup anymore and was happy just not to be in the same city as him. She had purchased a house in New Orleans and later got married. At first she decided to become a nurse and secured a job with Charity Hospital. That job did not last very long. On her first day of employment, she was told she had to clean and prepare the body of a man who had died during the night. No problem. She put on her gloves, her mask, then went to see about this cadaver. On a gurney was a body covered with a sheet, which she pulled back, and for the time in her life she stared at a dead person. She ran out of the room and quit her job that day. After that she went to work for the South Central Bell Telephone Company, and she would stay there for the rest of her employment days, retiring only because of declining health.

One day we were visiting with Joan Marie, and she said to us, "You know you don't work for Joe."

"Aaah, what do you mean?" I asked. "Of course we work for Joe."

"That's what I thought, too."

Joan Marie had been talking to some of the New Orleans–based singers we knew that had been in the business much longer than us. They hadn't heard good things about Joe, and whatever they didn't hear, Joan Marie explained to them. Their collective response was, "Why didn't you fire that son-of-a-bitch?" Joan Marie quickly understood that we had been conned into thinking Joe was in control of the Dixie Cups, but it was the other way around. Once Barbara and I understood it, we went back to the agents. Some of the agents felt sorry for us, noting, "We thought you guys knew that but just wanted to stay with him."

It was time to play the game smarter.

Legally, there was still a contract out there between Joe Jones and the Dixie Cups, and we wanted it negated. As always, Barbara and I were the polite ones, and we asked Joe to sign a cancellation, as we were no longer working together. This began endless rounds of "I'm going to get it to you soon. I'm going to get it to you next week. I'm going to get it to you next month." As long as the contract was in place, we didn't trust him.

Later in 1969 we got word that Joe Jones was going to be in New Orleans. We were talking to a cousin about our situation, and he suggested we call Joe and invite him to our house. This seemed like a good strategy, so Barbara telephoned, saying, "When you're in New Orleans, we want you to come to the house to talk with us about the contract situation." Joe was suspicious, asking why he had to go our mama's house. The answer was that it was quiet and we lived there. Joe suggested meeting at a bar, and we had to remind him that neither Barbara nor I hung out in bars. In the end he came to the house. Barbara and I set him at ease, and then our mother came into the room. He jumped up and said, "Hello, ma'am." "That's Mrs. Hawkins to you," she said sternly, and he looked over to me as if to say, What the heck did I walk into? He didn't know if my mother knew about how he had taken advantage of the Dixie Cups or how he sexually abused me. She didn't, as I never told her. She did know we were unhappy with Joe and felt mistreated, and that was enough for her. "I want my children's contract," she demanded.

Joe tried to dance away. "That's mine, it's not theirs."

"I'm giving you one month for you to get that contract in my hand."

"Well, what are you going to do about it?"

Barbara jumped into the conversation. She had been Joe's assistant in the Dixie Cups business all the time we had been in New York and knew some of the shady things he had done. She threatened to write it all out in a letter and then go to an attorney.

Joe tried to pass off the threat as a joke, but he knew Barbara had him. In the end, he gave the Dixie Cups a written termination letter.

That's when we started working with Ron Peters out of Fayetteville, North Carolina. He picked up the ball. Ron said, "I'm going to get you as much work as I possibly can. Don't worry about it." At that point it was just Barbara and I. We didn't sign with Ron. He was a good person, an honest person, and he worked our butts off. We just didn't have a contract with him.

We did think about recording again and discussed it with Ron, who said it was important first to get back out on the road so people could reacquaint themselves with the Dixie Cups, as we hadn't had a record in quite a while. Also we needed to make money. Ron never said it, but I believe he felt we would never be able to secure enough money independently to get back into the studio again.

Indeed, money was tight. When we moved back to New Orleans, we had a place to live, and that cut down on expenses. With the Joe Jones situation finally settled, we were getting bookings. It just was not enough income, so Barbara and I went to work. Barbara got a job with a minister who also owned a real estate company. She went back to school to become a real estate agent. It was a smart move, because real estate agents work independently, and if a job for the Dixie Cups came up, she could always rearrange her schedule. She brought me into the minister's office to work as a receptionist. Still, Barbara and I never gave up on the idea of being a Dixie Cup. In our hearts, we felt God had not brought us this far to leave us hanging.

By choice Barbara never married, and as I mentioned, I didn't either, although I have a son. Like all mothers, I thought my child was the most beautiful baby in the world. I was so convinced of that, I thought he would make a perfect baby model. I looked up an agency in the city and dialed the number. A woman named Hazel, who ran the agency, took my call and said to bring my baby down to the agency. After making nice to my gorgeous baby, she turned to me and said, "Oh, Rosa, you are such a beautiful girl. Have you ever thought about modeling, yourself?" Well, no, I hadn't. Earlier, I had told her about being a Dixie Cup, so she said, "I know you're not shy to be in front of people."

As it turned out, there could be no work for my son, because there were no agencies in Louisiana or the southern region that represented babies. If I wanted to pursue the baby modeling, Hazel could arrange something in Chicago. I said to her, "Hazel, thank you, but I don't like Chicago." The conversation turned back to me. "I'm going to send you on a 'go-see.'" It was for a sunglasses company, which was doing a layout in a magazine. They wanted to see a few girls. When I got there, they asked me to remove my sunglasses so they could see my eyes. I got the job.

I decided to take a course in modeling so I would know what I was doing when I was called for different jobs. I started with the Barbizon School of Modeling, which is still around, mostly helping young women begin a modeling career. I took a class, and when I graduated, the owner asked me if I would become an instructor. I said yes. After a while I realized I was teaching these girls how to get jobs but wasn't doing that for myself. I made the decision to put myself out there as well and made the rounds of the local agencies.

Once, after the Dixie Cups had performed at the French Quarter Festival in New Orleans, as I was coming off the stage, I kept hearing this person calling my name, "Rosa! Rosa! Rosa!" There were people around asking for autographs, and I couldn't figure where the voice was emanating from. Again, "Rosa! Rosa! It's me, Louellen." That caught my attention, and when I turned around and our eyes met, I realized this was a lady I'd worked for as a model many years before. Through her I had become the top Black model in New Orleans. Every time she received a job for a Black model, she would call me. She said to me, "It was something about you when you walked in my office. You had an attitude of humbleness, while at the same time showing you knew what you were doing."

When I started working with Louellen, there was at the time another young lady who had most of the Black modeling jobs in her pocket. For one of my first jobs, Louellen put me in a runway show with this other model. When I taught, I always told my girls don't ever peek between the curtains to see the person on the runway in front of you, because that could either boost or collapse your ego. I peeked at that girl, because she was the biggest news in Black modeling in the state, and when I saw her walk down the runway and do her turns, I said to myself, I can do that. When it was my turn, I went out on that runway and did what I had to do. I didn't flinch. From that point on, whenever Louellen had a runway gig, I was the one Black girl in the show unless she needed two or more girls.

I mostly did runway, as I wasn't comfortable with print photographers. I told Louellen, "I'm not pretty enough to do magazine photo modeling." The truth was, I wasn't that much of an exhibitionist. Sure, I could be on a runway and not have stage fright—I had been on various stages since I was a teenager. However, I never felt secure enough to scantily pose. Two things I didn't enjoy doing: posing for magazine layouts and having to appear in a two-piece bathing suit on the runway. The one time I was booked to do a bikini walk on a runway, I told Louellen I would do it only if I could wear something over it. Although I never made the covers of magazines as a model, photos and stories of the Dixie Cups have been in multitudes of newspapers and magazines, from *Rolling Stone* to *People*, so I don't think I missed anything.

Hazel's son worked with her, and he would also do some of the hiring. My weirdest booking came from him, and it arrived out of the blue. One day he called me saying he had a job if I was interested. He added, "I don't know if you'll take it, although you should trust me on this one." That got my attention. He explained, "There is a small convention in town, and the people in charge want to roast the boss. They'll pay you $700 [which was good money in those days], and you have about five lines to say." So far, so good. "Where is this convention going to be?" I asked. "Antoine's," he said.

That was a wow. Antoine's is one of the most famous restaurants not only in New Orleans but in the country. First opened in 1840, it pioneered such famous dishes as Oysters Rockefeller. The location was on St. Louis Street in the French Quarter. This was getting interesting. What was the drawback? The answer was I would have to dress like a hooker. First of all, the last thing I would ever do is dress like a prostitute, and even if I was so inclined, let's just say, I didn't have the clothes for it, which was my excuse. That got waved away.

Hazel's son said to me, "I know your sister is short, but you are skinny, so you could probably get into some of her clothes. The clothes would be tight and skimpy, and that would work." I said yes.

Not only did I borrow an outfit from Barbara, I went all in, taking one of her wigs as well. I did my makeup with double eyelashes and big, striking lipstick. This was New Orleans, and hookers weren't exotic creatures. Barbara gave me a ride down to the restaurant, laughing the whole time.

I guess I really looked the part, because when I arrived at Antoine's and went to open the door to walk in, the maître d' stopped me. "Where do you think you're going?" he asked in a not very friendly manner. So, I had to explain who I was. "You're the model for the banquet," he gasped. "Oh, my God." He let me in, but he didn't warn me about my greeting. I needed to use the ladies room, which meant walking through the whole restaurant. Heads turned. I even heard a few "I never..."

I headed for the ladies room on the upper floor, where I was going to hang my other clothes and add the last pieces of the outfit. At that moment some ladies from the restaurant came in. I shocked them. One woman said, "What are you doing here? I thought you came after the convention to clean up." Again I had to explain, "I'm not cleaning up tonight. They don't want everyone to know, but I'm the model that is going to roast your president." I put on Barbara's skirt, and about fifteen minutes later I was ready. They brought me out, and the president of the convention, when he saw me, his mouth dropped open. I moved to stand by him and said, "Hi, you remember me? How are you doing? Don't you remember me? You offered me dinner here tonight." He didn't know what to say, and then he glanced over to the side of the podium, where the men who set this up were laughing hysterically. At the end, I cleared everything up for the president and the audience, explaining that I was a model hired to help roast the president with this prank.

Now it was time for me to go home. Little did I know the navy had arrived. A ship had dropped anchor in the port of New Orleans, and many of them were on leave. I was standing in an alcove of the restaurant because I didn't want to stand on the street while waiting for my sister to pick me up. Bunches and bunches of sailors were passing by, whistling and yelling all sorts of profane things usually beginning with, "Oh, baby." The French Quarter is a horrible place to park, and I knew Barbara would be driving by, but every time I stepped out to see if she arrived, there were all sorts of propositions yelled to me. When my ride finally arrived, I jumped into the car as quickly as I could. Barbara said with a laugh, "You looked scared." I was, I said. And she answered, "I saw all those guys yelling at you and slowed down to watch the action." Sisters!

I continued working as a model until 2004. I also continued teaching, switching from Barbizon to the John Casablancas Centers. Like Barbizon, John Casablancas has been around for decades and has offices all over the United State and overseas.

I know what you're thinking—Rosa, you were a model. Didn't men ask you out? They did, but I wasn't looking for a mate. I had a son to raise, and my responsibility was to him.

CHAPTER ELEVEN

I'm Gonna Get You Yet

In 2003, when the district court decided in no uncertain terms that the Dixie Cups owned the copyright to the song "Iko Iko," Joe Jones quickly appealed. So Barbara, Joan Marie, and I had to return once again to the courts to defend our creation. In August of the same year, in the United States Court of Appeals for the Fifth Circuit, it was once again *Rosa Lee Hawkins, Barbara Anne Hawkins and Joan Marie Johnson vs. Joe Jones, dba Melder Publishing Company*, and once again we prevailed.

Here is one very telling paragraph from the decision:

> Jones has also claimed that he wrote "Iko Iko" on several occasions, including during cross examination testimony in this case. These statements are in direct contradiction to statements made by Jones in earlier sworn statements in previous litigation over the authorship of "Iko Iko." Jones introduced into evidence a 1968 settlement agreement claiming to release him for the obligation to pay plaintiffs in accordance with the 1965 songwriters' agreement. Plaintiffs all testified they did not sign the settlement agreement and that the signatures on the documents were forgeries. Plaintiffs also produced copies of several other district court opinions from cases in which Jones falsely claimed authorship of songs and attempted to use forged document as evidence.

Faked and forged documents!

Let's take a look at just one of the cases, *Johnson v. Tuff N Rumble Management Inc.*, which was really a lawsuit brought by Wardell Quezergue and Joseph "Smokey" Johnson, a former associate and Joe Jones band member, who sued Joe Jones dba Melder Publishing Co. for copyright infringement to the record "It Ain't My Fault." When the plaintiffs moved for summary judgment, it was contradicted by Joe, who filed two legal "oppositions." The court noted, "Jones's initial opposition included no evidence of a copyright assignment, and his supplemental opposition included a purported assignment from 1964 that was clearly prepared with modern word-processing equipment."

Joe ripped off not only the Dixie Cups but old friends as well, and he was clearly not above forging documents.

In our judicial proceeding, we moved to impose sanctions against Joe for bringing to the court a frivolous appeal. The court noted, "His [Jones's] only evidence in defense of plaintiffs-appellees' contract claims are a 1968 settlement agreement and a 1973 letter, both of which the jury believed to be forged documents."

The very weird idiosyncrasy about Joe Jones was that he could never bring himself to stop trying to do the Dixie Cups harm. He was like a dog with a bone, gnawing, gnawing, gnawing, and snapping at anyone who came within his eyesight. I'm not smart enough to question Joe's mind-set or even his sanity, but he could never let go of the need to inflict vengeance and punishment. It consumed him. For three decades he came at us in so many different ways, and in the end it took the full weight of the US judicial system to bring him back to reality.

When did the Joe Jones reign of terror start? Immediately after Barbara and I (Joan Marie had already left the group) decided we had had it with Joe and told him he needed to move all his stuff out of our apartment, including his bookcase, his piano, and his files. We took the key back to our apartment, and weeks afterward Barbara and I moved back to New Orleans. But this is how the meanness started. The first thing he did was steal our passports. It was an easy trick; the passports were in the files. He took them and wouldn't give them back. Then he wrote a nasty letter to the management of our apartment building, alleging all sorts of terrible things about us. The man who owned the apartment building wrote back to Joe, copying us as well. He basically said: "Why don't you leave these ladies alone? They don't want to have anything to do with you. I have suggested they return to New Orleans."

In New Orleans, in the early 1970s, we received from Joe a copy of a letter he sent to the Internal Revenue Service, again alleging all sorts of transgressions. The IRS ignored him. Later on he would write letters to New Orleans department stores where he figured we shopped, saying crazy things such as we owed him money and shouldn't be given a credit card.

Joe didn't come back to live in New Orleans. In the early 1970s, Barbara and I were at an event in the city, and we ran into one of the guys who played on the recordings of our single records and albums when we were at Red Bird and ABC-Paramount. He said to me, "Hey, you know our boy is no longer in New York."

I was more curious as to why than where, and the answer was the mob ran him out of town. To replace us, Joe would hang out in the clubs, meet some of the beautiful dancers, tell them of discovering the Dixie Cups, how he produced "Chapel of Love," and let them know he was in search of new talent. Some of the ladies took the bait. Nothing but sex ever happened between him and the girls. Not realizing his lesson from the Peppermint Lounge, that a lot of these clubs were mob-owned, he got on the wrong side of some of the wrong people. Word got out, and, in the end, so did Joe, who moved to Los Angeles.

During the 1970s he was always trying to find out which agents were booking us. As I mentioned, through the hard work of Ron Peters, we had steady gigs in North and South Carolina at colleges, state fairs, and then at military bases. I think we worked at just about every military base in the country. Joe found out Ron was getting us bookings. Ron at first ignored him. Joe, being crazily persistent, started contacting the colleges directly, saying if the Dixie Cups were hired, even at a fraternity, he would throw an injunction on them, as he owned the rights to the Dixie Cups name. Some of the colleges asked for proof about the ownership, and if that was the case, they would take us off the bill. Since he didn't have anything, the threat was discovered to be empty. Some colleges would call Ron asking who this crazy guy Joe Jones was. In the 1960s and 1970s, the music industry was a dirty business, with considerable mob involvement. What Joe didn't know was that Ron also had his contacts with the families. Ron didn't overtly fight Joe on anything, but Joe got the message and slipped away from challenging any bookings by Ron.

In the 1970s, as Barbara and I were trying to reestablish the Dixie Cups and also holding down other jobs, money was still very tight for us. Even with all these challenges from Joe Jones, we were reluctant to spend the money on an attorney. What we did have was ongoing idiocy. To avoid fighting Joe Jones every time we got a new gig somewhere, we decided to alter the name of the group to the Dixie Kups.

The new name caught the interest of the press. The *Tennessean Showcase* newspaper featured an Associated Press story that headlined, "Dixie Kups Girls Learn Business the Hard Way." This was the picturesque lead into the story: "Someone promised Barbara Hawkins a rose garden once and she even got to smell the flowers for a while. Then they wilted. Now she's trying to grow her own. . . . Now, 15 years later, the Hawkins sisters . . . have become the Dixi [sic]

Kups, singing the sweet old harmonies with a new third voice, Inell Young, and hoping for a comeback." Barbara was also quoted as saying, "I guess you could say we had problems. We had three gold records and we grossed a lot of money. But we never saw any of it. . . . We don't have a manager now, but we do have two lawyers—one to watch the other. We learned the hard way that the music business is about 10 percent music and about 90 percent business."

What's interesting is that in the interview, to avoid mentioning the problems with Joe Jones, we told a completely different story about the name change to the reporter, who wrote, "The group name is different now to avoid potential legal problems with the cup company after which it was originally named, but otherwise the Dixi Kups' act is probably not a lot different than in its heyday."

Earlier in 1978 a publication called the *Data News Weekly* reported: "The New Orleans Jazz & Heritage Festival will kick off aboard the S.S. *Admiral*, with the celebration headed by Allen Toussaint and joined by The Neville Brothers and The Dixi-Kups [sic]." Once again, we were telling a whole different story. The *Data News Weekly* writer reported we had formed our own production company, BERL Productions, and were planning a comeback. Once again Barbara was quoted, this time saying, "The Jazz and Heritage Festival has been good for the Dixie Cups as we had been getting a lot of calls for bookings and recordings since we started playing the festival three years ago." She was quoted as saying, "We always get a good reception here. The people like us because we are from home."

A news article from March 1985 boasted this headline: "Dixi-Kups: Old Songs Fuel 80's Comeback." Even worse, the writer wrote about Joe Jones as the Dixi-Kups' music director. We had changed the name to disassociate ourselves from him.

As it turned out, it was a very bad idea to become the Dixie Kups (or Dixi-Kups) for a number of reasons. First of all, it looked like a fake name. The booking agents came to us and said, "You don't have to do this. The Dixie Cups with that 'C' is the name you worked hard to establish. Joe Jones doesn't own anything, and you need to go back to using the original name." The biggest problem with the name change was that we inadvertently gave Joe more ammunition for his claim to the name the Dixie Cups, because he began to tell people, "If I didn't own the name, then why would they change their group name to the Dixie Kups?"

We went back to the Dixie Cups with the "C."

It was obvious that we needed to get a lawyer. Back in the days when Barbara was attending Southern University, back when she was getting arrested in a civil rights protest, she was manager of a real estate and insurance office and met a guy who was an attorney. She remembered him from the work he had done for the office and went to see him, telling him about this stone in our shoe that was causing our business to limp along, that we were having trouble moving forward. He represented us for a while. Whenever there was an injunction threat, he would write the college notifying them that Joe's papers were not legal papers. He always made the point that Joe never filed for ownership of the name, there was no date of legal action to the name, and never any legal file number listed. (Barbara and I own the name The Dixie Cups Incorporated.) Word eventually got out to the venues where groups like the Dixie Cups would play that these threats from Joe Jones were not to be taken seriously. We were able to fulfill our gigs.

If one of Joe's schemes was cut off, he would devise some other dastardly way to get at the Dixie Cups. He was a man possessed—and we were the objects of his obsessive behavior.

One day, out of the blue, I got a call from a friend in Las Vegas. "What's up," I asked in a friendly manner. And my friend said, "How can you come to Las Vegas and not tell me?"

"The Dixie Cups are going to be there?" I questioned. Neither the Dixie Cups nor I on a personal basis had a trip planned for Vegas. "I didn't know we're going to be in Las Vegas. Is it a show?"

"Yes, you're going to be with about six other girl groups at one of the casinos."

This was all news to me. "How did you know we're going to be there?"

"It was in the newspaper, a big advertisement." (She later faxed it over to us.)

"That's not us," I had to say to her. "We would have let you know if we were coming."

I made some phone calls to the casino and got in touch with show personnel, who assured me two of the Dixie Cups appearing at the casino were named Rosa and Barbara Hawkins.

We called our newest attorney in California and told him what was going on. He, in turn, called the casino. He told them something to the effect that these young ladies purporting to be the Dixie Cups—and we have no idea who they are—are not the real Dixie Cups. The real Dixie Cups own the copyright to the name, so if the casino introduces anyone as the Dixie Cups for a show, we will file suit, which we will win, because I am warning you that those girls are phonies with no rights to use the name.

My friend bought tickets to the show, wanting to see what would happen. She reported back to me saying that the emcee walked out on stage that night to tell the audience he had some bad news—the Dixie Cups were in a car accident and wouldn't be appearing.

Those fake Dixie Cups were a group of girls put together by Joe Jones.

In 1984 the city of New Orleans hosted the Louisiana World Exposition, a World's Fair of sorts. It was held one hundred years after the city's earlier try at global recognition, the World Cotton Centennial of 1884. As part of the celebration, the exposition invited as many New Orleans singers and musicians as it could find. Everyone I knew was getting a call—everyone except the Dixie Cups. I rang up the stage show organizers and introduced myself as Rosa Hawkins of the Dixie Cups to the receptionist who took the call. I said, "I'm calling because the exposition hasn't called us." She took a deep breath and then handed the phone off. A guy comes on and says, "We had you ladies down for two or three appearances, but your manager Joe Jones has written us a five-page letter," explaining that we didn't own the name the Dixie Cups, and we could not sing "Chapel of Love," because we were not the ones who owned the rights to the song, that we had stolen the song from him.

He continued, explaining that he talked to the lawyers, who said we needed to be scratched from the lineup. "Why would you do that?" I said. Of course, the answer was that Joe had threatened to sue if we appeared, and the lawyers decided to take the easy way out. One act out of many wasn't worth a fight. As a result, we were New Orleans born and bred, but we couldn't appear at our city's biggest extravaganza in our lifetime.

There was only one thing left to do—go back to the courts and prove once and for all that we owned the rights to the Dixie Cups name. Once again, the lawsuit was filed in New Orleans, and it was all the original Dixie Cups vs. Joe Jones.

This time it was a total mess-up on Joe's part. He arrived at the court without his lawyer. He brought with him boxes of papers, as if he had the legal library with him and he knew what he was doing. During the course of the trial, he whipped out some papers and put them on the judge's desk. The judge looked down at him and warned, "Please don't put that on my desk." Joe began to stutter. The judge cut him off: "I don't want it on my desk. If it was so important, someone would have officially filed to introduce it in court."

Joe's wife kept running out of the court looking for the lawyer. Things got weird and ugly for me. When I took the stand, Joe started asking me personal questions, particularly about my child. He asked, "And you have a son?"

I said, "Why are you asking me that?"

"I need his name."

"You don't need his name."

The judge stopped him in his tracks, asking, "Why do you need information on this young lady's son?"

Joe answered, "My case depends on it."

The judge continued, "But how? That child wasn't even born when the Dixie Cups were started."

"She had him out of wedlock. He was born in 1969."

"I don't know what you are trying to do, but it is not going to work. Whatever his name is, is his business and his mother's business."

Joe was trying to get to a point where he could accuse me of hooking up with the band leader on the *Shindig* tour of 1965. As I mentioned, my son was born in 1969, and he had nothing to do with the case. Joe was also trying to rattle me, which he did.

After that incident, I left the courtroom and just started crying. All the terrible things he did to me, the rape, the abuse, the mistreatment, everything was washing out of me in tears. Joan Marie came with me. She placed her hand on me, whispering, "Rosa Lee, you need to stop crying." Then she realized I wasn't crying because of what happened in the courtroom, I was crying because of what Joe Jones had done to me over the years we were in New York. I was dealing with stuff I had pushed down and down into the depth of my being. She quietly murmured, "I knew he was doing something, but I didn't know it was that bad. C'mon, Rosa Lee, he's not worth it." I must have cried for a half an hour. The lawyer didn't know if I was going to make it through the rest of the trial. I said to Joan Marie, "If he gets within two feet of me and says anything, I'm going to be going to jail."

Eventually his lawyer made an appearance, just when the jury was coming in with a verdict. The lawyer apologized and asked the court if he could cross-examine the Dixie Cups. The judge said no. Joe piped up, "That's not fair."

"You want to know what's not fair? You had my jury here since 9 a.m. this morning, and it is now the afternoon," the judge noted. "They have come back with a verdict."

"That's not right, because I have a lawyer here."

The judge said to the stenographer to make note in the court records what time the attorney walked in the door.

The jury found fully in our favor, and the judge reiterated that the Dixie Cups owned the rights to the name. After that Joe could no longer even pretend he had rights to the name Dixie Cups. We were finally free of Joe Jones!

Well, this is Joe Jones we're talking about. He did try once more.

The New Orleans Jazz & Heritage Festival has been around since 1970, expanding over the years to include all genres of music. It's a big platform, with concerts in multiple locations over a period of a few days. The event generally showcases many of the great New Orleans singers and musicians, from Dr. John and Fats Domino to the Neville Brothers and Irma Thomas, from Branford Marsalis to Harry Connick Jr. The Dixie Cups are regulars as well.

One year in the late 1980s or early 1990s, I don't recall the exact year, Joe was in town, and I guess he was bored, because he capriciously—and spitefully!—decided to stop the Dixie Cups from appearing at the JazzFest.

Maybe there was nothing on television that afternoon, and it was too early to sit at a bar. Anyway, Joe wrote a letter in longhand and sent it to the JazzFest offices by courier. It was the usual nonsense about him owning the name Dixie Cups and threatening a lawsuit. All of the ladies who work at the JazzFest knew us, and one called us to tell about the letter. We didn't really have to worry. The person in charge there also knew the Dixie Cups, and he called Joe, telling him he had three hours to get the same courier to deliver any legal papers he might have to substantiate his claim.

The JazzFest is still waiting.

CHAPTER TWELVE

When the Levee Breaks

Lizzie Douglas took the name Memphis Minnie, though she claimed in song to have been born in Algiers, Louisiana, and she was raised in Walls, Mississippi. The year was 1897, and by the time Memphis Minnie was ten, she could play the banjo, later switching to the guitar to play at local gatherings. Two years after the great Mississippi River floods of 1927, she and her husband, Kansas Joe (McCoy), recorded on Columbia Records the great blues number "When the Levee Breaks," which some forty years later was recorded by the rock group Led Zeppelin. And almost forty years after that, the song pretty much summed up what happened to New Orleans when a hurricane rose up out of the Gulf of Mexico and slammed into Louisiana. The opening lyrics are a beauty: "If it keeps on rainin,' levee's goin' to break / if it keeps on rainin,' levee's goin' to break / And the water gonna come in, have no place to stay." But a favorite line is deeper into the song, "Oh cryin' won't help you, prayin' won't do you no good."

When the hurricane hit New Orleans, we were on a tour bus, sitting toward the front. The driver was listening to the radio, and we heard something about a storm and our hometown, but with all the noise in the bus we couldn't distinguish the words and didn't completely understand what was said. We became worried for our families. This wasn't Hurricane Katrina. The year was 1965, and we were on the *Shindig* tour. The coming storm was Hurricane Betsy. Jimmy O'Neill, the *Shindig* host on the tour, always the gentleman, told Barbara, Joan

Marie, and me that he would try to get as much information as he could, and when we got to someplace with a phone, we could make a call.

Hurricane Betsy was a big storm that roared into New Orleans on September 9, 1965, breaching levees and inundating neighborhoods, particularly the lower Ninth Ward. It was the most significant hurricane to hit New Orleans until Hurricane Katrina in August 2005. Nothing happened to our mother's home, but the home of my oldest sister, Shirley, had water up to the light switches. This was a home my dad and Shirley's husband built and then had to abandon. Shirley didn't lose everything, which was what would eventually happen with Hurricane Katrina.

A study of hurricanes by the Massachusetts Institute of Technology reported that Louisiana was hit by 49 of the 273 hurricanes that made landfall on the American Atlantic Coast between 1851 and 2004. However, the oddity is that after Hurricane Betsy, New Orleans avoided direct hits by any storm until Hurricane Katrina, a period of forty years. The narrowest escape was the very powerful Hurricane Camille of 1969, which hit Louisiana, but it was small in diameter and fast moving. Most of the damage in the state was in Plaquemines Parish.

These hurricanes must have made an impression on my mother. When we left New York, we moved back in with our mom, and then about a year later we bought a big house in the Seventh Ward. We needed room for everyone, mother, Barbara, me, and my son. So we bought a four-bedroom (eleven rooms total), which was the biggest property on our side of the street in an integrated neighborhood. Our real estate agent at the time said to us, "I can't find no small house for you. You need a big house because you have big furniture." That same agent told us we didn't need to waste money on flood insurance, because the area of the city where we were buying had never flooded. As I noted, my mother lived in New Orleans through numerous hurricanes, and her recollections were probably dramatic, because she adamantly told the agent we wanted flood insurance.

The insurance did come in handy in the 1980s, when a non-hurricane storm caused localized flooding, and water seeped into our utility room and got into a cabinet where we stored 90 percent of our photos from Vietnam and most of the letters written to us by the soldiers. Insurance covered the damage. We still own the property.

When we first moved there, I had to figure out where my son was going to start his school years. I decided on private school, but those in the area were almost all of the Catholic denomination, and to get in you had to be Catholic and live in the parish. Demand was so strong that, as a new student, you wouldn't find out if you were on the roster until two days before the school year started. So I opted to put my son in the elementary school of Saint John's Lutheran, which was smaller than the others. Two boys we knew from our neighborhood also attended Saint John's Lutheran, but the older boy was graduating out, so my son and the other boy were the only two Black students.

When I would pick up my son from school, he would see the boys from Jesuit High School in New Orleans coming off buses or running to catch other buses. One day he said to me, "I want to go to Jesuit High School." I said, "Great, keep your grades up, and there is no reason you can't go there." In truth, there were plenty of reasons he might not make it to Jesuit High School. It was the best high school in the city, and predominantly white, and prospective students had to test to get in. Everyone, of course, reported to me how hard the tests were and how difficult for my son. He decided he wanted to start eighth grade at Jesuit High, so he took the entrance exam, which he aced, so well that he was accepted for the accelerated program, meaning he would be taking college-level courses. At graduation he was offered full academic scholarships to schools such as Louisiana State University, Baton Rouge; Marion Military Institute, Marion, Alabama; Vanderbilt University, Nashville; and Tulane University, New Orleans, but he opted to accept a full scholarship to Florida State University in Tallahassee.

I feel one of his major achievements was receiving the Magna Cum Laude Certificate of Honorable Merit from the American Classical League and the National Junior Classical League in the National Latin Exam.

He was a business major, and after graduation he didn't want to come back to New Orleans, because the job opportunities there were slim. He and his wife met in their second year of college. After they both graduated, they worked and two years later married. Two years after that, they had their first child, and four years later a second child. He decided to stay in Florida and took a job in Tampa. (Barbara never had children, but she adopted a little girl, who after graduation joined the navy in 2004. She earned a bachelor of arts in law from Keiser University in Tampa in 2018.)

My son wanted us to relocate to Tampa. I resisted because our mother had been ill, and you just can't move the elderly, pull them out of a familiar environment where they knew their doctors, ministers, and caregivers. These were people she depended on. Our mother passed in 2003.

The next year Barbara and I moved, but not to Florida. After thirty-one years in the old home, we bought a two-story house in New Orleans East. We didn't rent out the old home, because it had structural issues. Barbara and I learned a real estate lesson from our mother; when we bought our new house, we were sure to take flood insurance, although just like thirty years before, the real estate agent assured us this new neighborhood had never flooded.

Before Katrina was even a blink on the radar, we decided to renovate the new house, including floors, windows, and plumbing.

Hurricane Katrina didn't aim directly for New Orleans; it meandered. On August 23 it was over the Bahamas and then hit Florida before reemerging in the Gulf of Mexico, where it intensified. On August 29 it slammed into the southern coast lands of Mississippi and Louisiana. People had time to watch, wait, prepare, and, if you were in Gulfport, Mississippi, or New Orleans, worry.

We were paying attention but not doing what we needed to do when a hurricane approached. There was a loose kind of plan in place. If Aaron Neville was on the road and a storm was approaching, he would call his agency to get rooms in a safe location away from Louisiana for his wife and family. Barbara and I were in that group of family. Aaron and his wife, Joel, had four children and eventually grandchildren. We lived about five minutes away from Aaron and Joel. With Katrina looking like it was headed toward Louisiana, Joel called Barbara to let her know they were forming a caravan of cars heading north to Tennessee. We were already preparing for the storm. We didn't like to drive our car out of the state, so Barbara got a rental car at the airport and left our car there. I was home dealing with the plumber. The weather was beginning to turn when I get a call about four o'clock from Joel asking where the heck were Barbara and I. An excited Joel was telling me she had talked with Barbara, saying we were going to leave town at four o'clock. In the caravan was her family, but one son was still in New Orleans. Joel forgot to tell us about her son starting out later than her, which was important, because Barbara was stuck in traffic trying to get back from the airport.

I moved a lot of personal things to the second floor, and when Barbara finally arrived, we started packing the car—important documents, jewelry, and enough clothes for a few days. I had never driven to Tennessee, and now the interstate was jammed with other people doing the same thing as Barbara and I. We struggled with progress as the forward rains began to hit the state. At Baton Rouge I called Brian, a close friend of my son's, whom we knew for decades. When he answered I asked if he had room. When he said yes, I got off the interstate and headed to his house. The normal two-minute ride took about twenty minutes. We tried to call my son, but many of the cell networks were down. We later found out "Little Aaron" Neville was coming up behind us with a smaller group of cars. If we had known, we would have joined them. Instead, we decided to stay in Baton Rouge. We couldn't make contact with my son, and then, bingo! He, because he couldn't get us directly, gave a call to Brian to see whether he had heard from us—and there we were.

All you had to do was turn on the television to see New Orleans underwater and people scrambling to survive. According to subsequent studies, over fifty of the city's levees were breached, flooding most of the city as well as neighboring parishes. By one estimate almost a thousand fellow citizens from Louisiana died in the hurricane. In the middle of it all and the immediate aftermath, it was hard to learn what was happening to our small properties. Sometimes I would watch the news, and the reporters would place the street where we had moved to one year before in the center of Katrina. Other news stories reported that area of the city dry. We couldn't tell if the storm hit us or not. You had to find someone still there and ask what the heck happened to our house. We had some friends still in New Orleans. One woman we knew who made her living in real estate as a home flipper told us if she could get down to our house, she would call back, but the city was so flooded that it took her a whole week before she could get into the area.

We stayed in Baton Rouge for two weeks. We eventually left because my son wanted us in Florida. Even weeks after the hurricane, the roads were crowded. What used to be an eight-hour drive ended up being almost a fifteen-hour drive.

We stayed in Tampa, living in a hotel for almost a year. We couldn't even move in with my son, because he had just bought a home, which was still being built, and he and his family were living with his in-laws. It was a very long year. Breakfast at the IHOP and dinner with my son's in-laws, who fed us every night. There was so much uncertainty in our lives, not knowing if the house we had bought was still standing, what happened to friends and family—if their homes were still standing.

Our friend who dabbled in real estate finally made it down to our old house and took some pictures. It had been underwater, but the building was still standing. This was the house where my son grew up. As to the house that we had just bought, the water came over the driveway and into the house. As I mentioned, I had put a lot of stuff upstairs. As the storm approached, we bought these large bins and put all books, papers, and much of stuff we didn't need immediately into the containers, which were on the second floor. Over half of the roof came off the house, and Barbara's bedroom was badly damaged. The items in the containers were saved. The National Guard was protecting the area from looters. When we finally came back to pack stuff up, we had to show IDs. There was still no electricity or water in the area.

As for our old house, from the outside, you couldn't tell it had been underwater unless you looked to see the water line. It was a sturdy structure made of brick with a stucco exterior. While it didn't crumble, the whole area had been flooded out. It was heartbreaking, as this was the house where I raised my child and took care of my mom. It was a big house, and the band members for the Dixie Cups used to come by to practice. The den was large enough to have them all set up. For many, many years, we practiced at that house. Mother would come home from the senior citizen center, sit down, and enjoy the practice sessions. When individual band members heard we were going to tear the house down, each one in his own way passed by the house and stood out front to say goodbye to the structure. Not having the house there was a bit much for everybody.

We still own the property. We can sell it if we want to. Indeed, we have had hundreds of offers. Everyone wanted it cheap or cheaper. You couldn't blame them for trying. Many of my neighbors got rid of their properties for $10,000 or $15,000 as quickly as possible and moved on.

We sold the two-story house we'd moved into a year before the hurricane, because it was taking too long to get the area back up and livable. There was no electricity, water, or sewage for a very long time. FEMA (the Federal Emergency Management Agency) visited us, saying they could give us a trailer to stay in for six weeks. That was a bit dangerous, because criminals were snatching trailers from people right and left. A young lady bought the house, gutted the whole place, and rebuilt. I didn't want to do it. After we came back and saw the changes to the neighborhood, it was full of strangers in the area who were not living there before Katrina hit, and even stranger people watching the empty houses, ready to steal or worse. We were the last ward in the state to get electricity and water. Who wanted to stay in there?

Aaron Neville's house also went under the waters. He and Joel lived in Tennessee for a while. She has since passed away.

My older sister, Shirley, raised five boys. Two became policemen, one a professor at a Missouri college, and two went into the military. She lived in the same home since her children were small. I liked to say she cooked and cleaned for seven men—her five kids, her husband, and our father. It was an old, sturdy house, but her area went under the waters as well. For a long time, no one could get back to that part of the city. Finally, one of her sons, who was a policeman, journeyed back there to see if the house was all right. He called me later that day and said my sister shouldn't come down to look at the place. During the hurricane, the neighbor's house said, "Well, let me see how Miss Shirley is doing, because I don't see her, the kids, or the grandkids." So the neighbor's house traveled over to my sister's property to see what was going on. That, in reality, is what happened. The neighbor's house was pushed off its foundation by the flooding waters, slammed into Shirley's house, and shoved it off its own foundation and halfway off the lot. When the marshals went into the area, they put orange "X's" on every part of the house, because it was askew and very unsafe. No one could go in. Shirley didn't like to go to concerts, because she was uncomfortable in crowds, so she would never come to see us sing, but she was very loyal to Barbara and me. Shirley kept what she called her Dixie Cups wall: every newspaper or magazine article, every photograph, every review about us she would cut out and tape up on the wall. She wasn't allowed back in the house. She couldn't get her papers, her family pictures, furniture, pots and pans. Everything, including the Dixie Cups wall, was gone from her. Today, she lives in a condo in New Orleans with her youngest son.

We had been looking for Joan Marie, because we didn't know what happened to her during or after the storm. Finally, we got a call from her. She had moved to Texas before the hurricane. I said to her, "Why didn't you call us? You could have come here with Barbara and me." She teased, "Are you crazy, Rosa Lee? We lived together for five years. And that's five years I don't want to relive." Oh, she could make me laugh. Although she had been in Texas, she didn't give up her home in New Orleans and was luckier than most. Her house had some flood damage, but not severe. She had become a Jehovah's Witness, and "brothers" from her church had come to her home and made it livable again.

Many of the older New Orleans musicians of my generation dispersed after the hurricane. Even some of the Dixie Cups' band members moved away. Most of our neighbors, such as those near to the two-story house we had acquired, were gone, never to come back. A lot of people departed because it was easier to leave the devastation than it was to fight with the government. To get money from FEMA that was due you as a citizen of the United States and as a taxpayer of Louisiana was time-consuming and seemingly impossible. They would put you through the wringer. You had to be smart to live in that city after the hurricane and had to know how to deal with the government because you had to argue with the people FEMA brought in who didn't know anything about New Orleans. Barbara and I came out fine, because we learned from our mother to always get flood insurance. As for FEMA, I never got a dime from that agency.

I was born in New Orleans, spent my childhood and school years there. After we recorded "Chapel of Love," Barbara and I moved to New York for five years. Then it was back to New Orleans for more than thirty-five years. Hurricane Katrina arrived, and we couldn't live in the city anymore. At first we thought we would end up in Tennessee, near Aaron and Joel, but my son strongly urged us to come to Florida. What can I say? His argument was, "We really need to see you here." It was emotional. So Barbara and I packed up everything we owned and came to live in Tampa.

One day my youngest grandchild came by the townhouse Barbara and I were thinking of acquiring as our next home. He said to me, "Are you gonna move in here?"

I said, "We're thinking about it."

He looked around and said, "I don't think you ought to live here."

My heart dropped. "Why, you don't want me here?" I asked.

He answered, "I don't think this will be good for you."

I was on the verge of tears until my son pulled me over. "You're missing the big picture, Mom. By you living here, you are taking away a vacation trip from him. He doesn't have to pack a bag to go see Grandma Rosa."

CHAPTER THIRTEEN

Little Bell

On September 20, 2005, a huge concert, The Big Apple to the Big Easy, took place in Madison Square Garden to raise funds for the Hurricane Katrina relief efforts. Stars from around the globe, but most importantly from New Orleans, gathered in New York to help attract donations for victims of the flooding. Along with the likes of Elton John, Cyndi Lauper, John Fogerty, Jimmy Buffett, Bette Midler, Elvis Costello, and Simon & Garfunkel were a slew of New Orleans performers, including Allen Toussaint, the Neville Brothers, the Dixie Cups, Irma Thomas, Dave Bartholomew, Buckwheat Zydeco, and Clarence "Frogman" Henry. As a *New York Times* columnist noted in the paper two days later:

> Although the city has been devastated, its musicians persevere. The headliners . . . helped fill the $500 seats. . . . But the musicians from New Orleans—among them the Neville Brothers, the original Meters, Irma Thomas, Kermit Ruffins, and the Dirty Dozen Brass Band—out-sang and out-funked most of the better-known stars. The programming was smart: New Orleans musicians had the first and last words, in the form of parade music from the Rebirth Brass Band. New Orleans music, from jazz to hip-hop (which wasn't represented at the concert), has a distinctive rolling swing that's directly derived from community celebrations. It's deeply connected to Mardi Gras songs (like "Iko Iko" and "Brother John," which

the Dixie Cups sang on Tuesday night, and "Hey Pocky Way" performed by the Meters and the Neville Brothers) and brass-band music for funerals and parades.

After Hurricane Katrina, Barbara and I found ourselves being part of the entertainment set trying to help bring in financial aid. In regard to the latter, being participants at The Big Apple to the Big Easy concert was one of the treasured moments of our career as the Dixie Cups. For one thing, a couple of notables were there to introduce the acts, people like actor Paul Newman and former president Bill Clinton. Both came over to personally greet us and to say how much they loved our music. President Clinton's greeting was special. I had asked his security guard if it was OK to say hello when he came off the stage. The guard whispered, "Oh, that's no problem, as he loves the songs of the Dixie Cups." I was sure the guard was saying that to me just to be nice, but then there was President Clinton coming down the steps from the stage. We introduced ourselves. He said, "I know who you are, and I love your music." He started singing "Chapel of Love." For me, it meant a helluva lot that a president of the United States would know your name as an entertainer and know your music.

So many musicians were very kind to us. Cyndi Lauper, when she saw us, she literally gasped. "Oh my God," she said. "The Dixie Cups, you're so beautiful." Indeed, one of the high points of the show was the Dixie Cups. We sang "Chapel of Love," and then Irma Thomas and Cyndi Lauper joined us for a rousing version of "Iko Iko." By the time the song was over, everyone in Madison Square Garden was on their feet. Immediately afterward we had to fight our way to the dressing room, as everyone wanted to congratulate us. Then the absolute topping was a call from my son, who had watched the show at his house. "Ma," he said, and I could tell he had tears of joy in his eyes, "you were awesome. I used to come to your show, but this was ...," and he couldn't find another word. "This was so awesome." Then he put my grandson on the phone, and he said, "Grandma Rosa, you were so pretty. Why didn't you bring me to New York?" That was a night I could never relive. I was on cloud nine.

I should add that the third Dixie Cup was Athelgra Neville, who is the sister to the Neville Brothers and Barbara's close friend since they were teenagers. After Joan Marie retired, our first regular Dixie Cup was Beverly Brown. As I mentioned, she also suffered poor heath and died very young, back in the mid-1980s. We tried other women, who didn't work out. I suggested to Barbara that we ask Athelgra. She didn't think she could sing, but Barbara and I knew she could. Athelgra has been the third Dixie Cup for over twenty years.

In recent years, when a New Orleans singer has died, whether it's Fats Domino, Dr. John, Ernie K-Doe, and even Aaron's wife, Joel, there has been the traditional second line, which I'll explain. In New Orleans, for a brass-band funeral parade, the main section, actually those who have a permit to parade (usually with the brass band) is the first line. Those who follow the brass band, the mourners or those who just want to enjoy the music, constitute the second line. On October 3, 2016, Joan Marie Johnson died, but there was no second line for her. She had become a Jehovah's Witness, and she had a quiet service. Barbara attended, but I didn't. I don't like going to funerals. The only funeral I willingly went to was my mother's. I don't like seeing anyone in a box. Instead, I like to remember that person from the last time I saw him or her in life. Strange how those of us in the entertainment industry long past our prime and hit-making years are still remembered so eloquently and affectionately. It was no different for Joan Marie. She had left the Dixie Cups in 1966, and fifty years later when she departed the realm of the living, she was still news. Barbara, the usual spokesperson for the Dixie Cups, was interviewed about Joan Marie by numerous news outlets, including the *New York Times*, and *Billboard* magazine, which picked up an Associated Press story, ran a quote from Barbara:

> Joan Marie Johnson, one of the founding members of the New Orleans girl group The Dixie Cups, who had a No. 1 hit in 1964 with "Chapel of Love," has died at a hospice in New Orleans. She was 72. Johnson, who was only with the group for its first few years because she was diagnosed with sickle cell anemia, died of congestive heart failure October 3, according to former bandmate Barbara Ann Hawkins.

The first I heard of the group MusiCares was around the time of Ernie K-Doe's funeral in 2001. MusiCares is a nonprofit organization incorporated in 1993 by the National Academy of Recording Arts and Sciences, which has over the years provided more than $60 million in health, financial and rehabilitation resources to music people in times of need. Ernie K-Doe boasted one huge hit, the #1 recording in 1961 of the song "Mother-in-Law," but he was the quintessential New Orleans singer: flamboyant, entertaining, and a big promoter of his hometown. When he died, the city of New Orleans wanted to have his body lie in state at the old Governor's Mansion, and MusiCares stepped in to help pay expenses. The group would step in to help Barbara and me as well.

After Hurricane Katrina we eventually made our way to Tampa, but in the months after the hurricane when various groups were tracking missing people, our name came up as missing. My son was watching the news when he read a banner from the Associated Press that asked, "Does anyone know where the Dixie Cups are?" MusiCares was also trying to track down all the New Orleans singers and musicians that were either killed or dispersed by the hurricane. Apparently, we were on that list.

We lived in a hotel for about a year, subsidized by FEMA, but it wasn't a good fit. I couldn't take it anymore. I was having anxiety attacks. So we moved into an apartment, and MusiCares paid for the first six months. Around the end of 2006, Barbara and I bought a townhouse in a new development, which is where we still live. On our walls and shelves are numerous awards, certifications, and trophies given to us for our contributions to the world of music. There are important ones, like being inducted into the Rhythm & Blues Hall of Fame and the Vocal Group Hall of Fame. Our hometown of New Orleans and the state of Louisiana have bestowed innumerable awards on us, such as making the Dixie Cups Grand Marshal of the Mardi Gras parade, inducting us into the Louisiana Treasures Hall of Fame, and the fun one of having a star on the New Orleans Walk of Fame at Tipitina's. The renowned music venue, formerly housing the 501 Club at Napoleon and Tchoupitoulas Streets, opened in 1977 to honor R&B pianist and New Orleans mainstay Professor Longhair, who once recorded a song called "Tipitina." Almost every singer who visits New Orleans plays there, and some, like the Dixie Cups, are on the Walk of Fame.

We also made the mail. In 2005 a plaque bearing a reproduction of an actual envelope with our photo reads: "The New Orleans Jazz and Heritage Foundation Inc. in association with the United States Postal Service is proud to present the Official Commemorative Envelope for the 36th Anniversary of the New Orleans Jazz and Heritage Festival to Rosa L. Hawkins of The Dixie Cups." (Similar awards went to Barbara and Athelgra).

Barbara and I have lived in Tampa for over a decade now. Do we miss New Orleans? I have to be frank. Even before Hurricane Katrina, after my mother died, New Orleans lost its gloss for me. If Katrina hadn't hit, maybe I would still be there. But maybe not, as my son and two grandkids live here in Tampa. I'm very content here. For Barbara, it is different. I know Barbara's body may reside in Tampa, but her heart is not here. It's in New Orleans.

NOTES

Chapter One: Sugah Wooga

Page 6 "I was just beginning to have..." David Ritz, *The Brothers Neville* (Boston: Little, Brown, 2000), 71–72.
Pages 8–9 "I sang it from the heart..." Ritz, *Brothers Neville*, 97.

Chapter Two: You Talk Too Much

Page 17 "Immediately after the session..." Jeff Hannusch, *I Hear You Knockin': The Sound of New Orleans Rhythm and Blues* (Ville Platte, LA: Swallow, 1985), 75.
Page 17 "He formed the band..." Joe Jones (1926–2005), Spectropop Remembers, www.spectropop.com/remembers/joejones.htm.
Page 18 "Paul Gayten, a Californian, recorded..." Larry Birnbaum, *Before Elvis: The Prehistory of Rock 'n' Roll* (Lanham, MD: Scarecrow Press, 2013), 319.
Page 18 "He [Joe Jones] talked his way..." Joe Jones, You Talk Too Much, www.onehitwondersthebook.com/?page_id=7924.
Page 19 "when Roy Brown came to..." Joe Jones, You Talk Too Much, www.onehitwondersthebook.com/?page_id=7924.
Page 20 "In 1952, Cosimo Matassa played..." Birnbaum, *Before Elvis*, 331–32.

Chapter Three: Marie Laveau

Page 24 "After the War..." Rick Coleman, *Blue Monday: Fats Domino and the Lost Dawn of Rock 'n' Roll* (Cambridge, MA: Da Capo Press, 2006), 22.
Page 24 "By the age of twelve..." Coleman, *Blue Monday*, 39–40.

Chapter Four: Thank You Mama, Thank You Papa

Page 43 "There you could write a song..." Alan Betrock, *Girl Groups: The Story of a Sound* (New York: Delilah Books, 1982), 39.

Page 47 "When Leiber mentioned..." Ken Emerson, *Always Magic in the Air* (New York: Penguin Books, 2005), 43.

Chapter Five: Chapel of Love

Page 51 "The New Orleans lilt..." Ken Emerson, *Always Magic in the Air: The Bomp and Brilliance of the Brill Building Era* (New York: Penguin Books, 2005), 218.

Page 52 "considered by *Billboard* magazine..." Billboad Staff, 100 Greatest Girl Group Songs of All Time: Critics Picks, https://www.billboard.com/articles/columns/pop/7857816/100-greatest-girl-group-songs.

Page 52 "According to Ken Emerson, the success of 'Chapel of Love'..." Emerson, *Always Magic in the Air*, 218.

Page 59 "Finger snaps, light horn riffs..." Dave Marsh, *The Heart of Rock & Soul: The 1001 Greatest Singles Ever Made* (New York: New American Library, 1989), 194.

Page 59 "Spector took two cracks..." 500 Greatest Songs of All Time, *Rolling Stone*, https://www.rollingstone.com/music/music-lists/500-greatest-songs-of-all-time-151127/u2-one-70151/.

Chapter Nine: Iko Iko

Page 111 "'Jock-a-Mo' came from two songs..." Jeff Hannusch, *I Hear You Knockin': The Sound of New Orleans Rhythm and Blues* (Ville Platte, LA: Swallow, 1985), 262.

DISCOGRAPHY

(Red Bird & ABC-Paramount)

Red Bird Records

Albums

Chapel of Love, 1964
Iko Iko, 1965
The Best of the Dixie Cups, 1966

Singles/EPs

Chapel of Love/Ain't That Nice (RB 10-001), 1964
People Say/ Girls Can Tell (RB 10-006), 1964
You Should Have Seen the Way He Looked at Me/No True Love (RB 10-012), 1964
Little Bell/Another Boy Like Mine (RB 10-017), 1964
(EP) The Dixie Cups/Jersey Red (RBEV 28001), 1964
(EP) The Dixie Cups/The Jelly Beans (RBEV 28002), 1964
(EP) The Dixie Cups, You Should Have Seen the Way He Looked at Me (RBEV 28006), 1964
Iko Iko/Gee Baby Gee (RB 10-024), 1965
Geethe Moon Is Shining Bright/I'm Gonna Get You Yet (RB 10-032), 1965

ABC-Paramount

Albums

Riding High (LP-ABCS-525), 1965

Singles

Two-Way-Poc-A-Way/That's Where It's At (45-10692), 1965
What Comes Up Must Come Down/I'm Not That Kind of Girl (To Marry) (45-10715), 1965
A-B-C Song/That's What the Kids Said (45-10755, 1965
(ABC Records) Love Ain't So Bad (After All)/Daddy Said No (45-10855), 1966
*Numerous collectible, oldies, compilation, re-releases and small-label recordings starting in the 1970s and beyond. The group also released a non-label CD/album *Doing It Our Way* in 2011.

SELECTED BIBLIOGRAPHY

Books

Betrock, Alan. *Girl Groups: The Story of a Sound*. New York: Delilah Books, 1982.
Birnbaum, Larry. *Before Elvis: The Prehistory of Rock 'n' Roll*. Lanham, MD: Scarecrow Press, 2013.
George, Nelson. *The Death of Rhythm & Blues*. New York: Pantheon Books, 1988.
Coleman, Rick. *Blue Monday: Fats Domino and the Lost Dawn of Rock 'n' Roll*. Cambridge, MA: Da Capo Press, 2006.
Emerson, Ken. *Always Magic in the Air: The Bomp and Brilliance of the Brill Building Era*. New York: Penguin Books, 2005.
Hannusch, Jeff. *I Hear You Knockin': The Sound of New Orleans Rhythm and Blues*. Ville Platte, LA: Swallow, 1985.
Harris, Sheldon. *Blues Who's Who: A Biographical Dictionary of Blues Singers*. New York: Arlington House, 1989.
Marsh, Dave. *The Heart of Rock & Soul: The 1001 Greatest Singles Ever Made*. New York: New American Library, 1989.
Ritz, David. *The Brothers Neville*. Boston: Little, Brown, 2000.
Smith, Steve. *Rock Day by Day*. Enfield, Great Britain: Guinness Books, 1987.
Spector, Ronnie, with Vince Waldron. *Be My Baby: How I Survived Mascara, Miniskirts and Madness or My Life as a Fabulous Ronette*. New York: Harmony, 1990.
Ward, Ed. *Rock of Ages: The Rolling Stone History of Rock & Roll*. New York: Rolling Stone Press, 1986.
Whitburn, Joel. *Top 40 Hits*. New York: Billboard Books, 1989.

Newspapers

I, along with my sister Barbara, have long clipped newspaper articles about our career. Unfortunately, we often didn't include the name and date of the publication. What information I have, I included with quotations within the book.

Internet

Joe Jones (1926–2005), Spectropop Remembers, www.spectropop.com/remembers/joe Jones.htm

Joe Jones/You Talk Too Much, The Golden Hits of the 60s, www.onehitwondersthebook.com/?page_id=7924

Joe Jones Singer, Wikipedia, https://en.wikipedia.org/wiki/Joe_Jones_(singer)

Sam Roberts, "Harold Battiste, Musician, Mentor and Arranger Dies at 83," *New York Times*, June 26, 2015, https://www.nytimes.com/2015/06/26/arts/music/harold-battiste-musician-mentor-and-arranger-dies-at-83.html

Richard Skelly, "Artist Biography," ALLMUSIC, https://www.allmusic.com/artist/harold-battiste-jr-mn0000669385/biography

Willie Tee, Wikipedia, https://en.wikipedia.org/wiki/Willie_Tee

John Parales, "Willie Tee, New Orleans Musical Innovator Dies at 83," *New York Times*, September 13, 2007, https://www.nytimes.com/2007/09/13/arts/music/13turbinton.html

Jeff Hannusch, "Masters of Louisiana Music: Earl Silas Johnson IV (Earl King)," *Offbeat Magazine*, http://www.offbeat.com/articles/masters-of-louisiana-music-earl-silas-johnson-iv-earl-king/

Uncle Dave Lewis, "Artist Biography," ALLMUSIC, https://allmusic.com/artist/oscar-papa-celestin-mn0001574169/biography

"Dr. Joseph M. Brenner, Practiced Internal Medicince 44 years," Obituaries Today, *New Orleans Times-Picayune*, August 5, 2012, https://www.nola.com/news/2012/08/dr_joseph_m_brenner_practiced.html

Sylvia Robinson, Wikipedia, https://en.wikipedia.org/wiki/Sylvia_Robinson

Songs Written by Jerry Leiber, Music VF.com, https://www.musicvf.com/songs.php?page=artist&artist=Jerry+Leiber&tab=songaswriterchartstab

Bruce Eder, "Artist Biography," https://www.allmusic.com/artist/george-goldner-mn0000648075

"Why Don't They Let Us Fall in Love," Wikipedia, https://en.wikipedia.org/wiki/Why_Don%27t_They_Let_Us_Fall_in_Love

Billboard Staff, 100 Greatest Girl Group Songs of All Time: Critics' Pick, *Billboard*, February 10, 2017, https://www.billboard.com/articles/columns/pop/7857816/100-greatest-girl-group-songs

The Big Tenth Thank You, ABC-Paramount, *Billboard*, September 18, 1965, https://www.americanradiohistory.com/Archive-Billboard/60s/1965/Billboard%201965-09-18.pdf

Peter Lindblad, Book Review: "Peppermint Lounge: The Mob, the Music, and the Most Famous Dance Club of the '60s," Backstage Auctions Inc., https://backstageauctions.blogspot.com/2012/10/book-review-peppermint-lounge-mob-music.html

Iko Iko Explained, https://everything.explained.today/Iko_Iko/

Helen Brown, "The Mysterious Origins of Iko Iko," *Financial Times*, July 24, 2017, https://www.ft.com/content/b5892a0a-6179-11e7-8814-0ac7eb84e5f1

Rosa Lee Hawkins, Barbara Anne Hawkins, Joan Marie Johnson, v. Joe Jones, United States Court of Appeals for the Fifth Circuit, August 29, 2003, http://www.ca5.uscourts.gov/opinions/unpub/02/02-30473.0.wpd.pdf

IKO IKO – Meaning of the Real Words and Their Origins, https://www.youtube.com/watch?v=Hj6-irrsnsw&t=137s

Selected Bibliography

Matt Reynolds, "EMI Sued for Dixie Cups' 'Iko Iko' Royalties," *Courthouse News Service*, July 25, 2017, https://www.courthousenews.com/emi-sued-dixie-cups-iko-iko-royalties/

Shivaree, http://groovytunesday.com/descriptions/misc/shivaree.html

A Rock n' Roll Historian, Shindig Tour 1965, February 11, 2017, https://rnrhistorian.blogspot.com/2017/02/shindig-tour-1965.html

A Rock n' Roll Historian, Summer 1964 Caravan of Stars, March 3, 2014, https://rnrhistorian.blogspot.com/2014/03/summer-1964-caravan-of-stars.html

Vietnam War Allied Troop Levels 1960–73, http://www.americanwarlibrary.com/vietnam/vwatl.htm

Barbara McCarragher, Hurricanes: History, http://web.mit.edu/12.000/www/m2010/teams/neworleans1/hurricane%20history.htm

Joan Brunkard, Gonza Namulanda, Raoult Ratard, "Hurricane Katrina Deaths, Louisiana, 2005," *Disaster Medicine and Public Health Preparedness* 2, no. 4 (April 8, 2013): 215–23, https://www.cambridge.org/core/journals/disaster-medicine-and-public-health-preparedness/article/hurricane-katrina-deaths-louisiana-2005/8A4BA6D478C4EB4C3308D7DD48DEB9AB

John Parales, "Rolling Rhythms to Beat the Bayou Blues," *New York Times*, September 22, 2005, https://www.nytimes.com/2005/09/22/arts/music/rolling-rhythms-to-beat-the-bayou-blues.html

Associated Press, "Joan Marie Johnson Co-Founder of the Dixie Cups Dies at 72," *Billboard*, October 12, 2016, https://www.billboard.com/articles/news/7541035/joan-marie-johnson-dixie-cups-obit

Recording Academy MUSICARES, https://www.grammy.com/musicares

INDEX

A&M College, 38
ABC-Paramount Records (ABC Records), 68–72, 127
"A-B-C Song," 59
"Adam Bit the Apple," 19
Adams, Faye, 20
Ad Lib Club, 83, 84
Ad-Libs, the, 49, 68
Adorns, the, 73
AFO Records, 6
"Ain't She Sweet," 64
"Ain't That a Shame," 8
"Ain't That Nice," 62
Aladdin Records, 20
Albert, Don, 18
Alexander, Rev. Avery, 29, 39
Ali, Muhammad, 94
"All Day and All of the Night," 83
Allen, Lee, 18, 20
All Platinum Records, 40
"All Grown Up," 63
"All These Things," 8
"Always a First Time," 41
Always Magic in the Air: The Bomp and Brilliance of the Brill Building Era, 47
American Bandstand, 83
American Broadcasting-Paramount Theatres, 68

American Federation of Musicians Local 1496, 6, 19
American Folk Blues Festival, 83
Amy Vanderbilt Complete Book of Etiquette, 31
Andrews Sisters, 69
Angels, the, 45
Animals, the, 87
Anka, Paul, 68
"Another Boy Like Mine," 63, 110
Antoine's, 121
Apollo Theater, 93
Armstrong, Louis, 59
Arthur, 59
Astronauts, the, 11
Atlantic Records, 45, 68
Atomic Rebops, 16, 17
"At the Hop," 68

"Baby I Love You," 44
Bacharach, Burt, 43
"Back in My Arms Again," 72
Baker, Mickey, 40
Ballard, Florence, 79
Banks, Bessie, 49
Barbizon, 31, 120, 123
"Barefootin'," 66
Barnes, Eula Lee, 4, 5

Barry, Jeff, 43, 44–46, 48–52, 53, 62–68, 107, 108, 110
Bartholomew, David, 7, 8, 18, 20, 24, 41, 101, 141
Bates, Vivian, 37, 40, 71
Batiste, David, 101
Battiste, Harold, 5, 6, 7, 8, 18, 20, 101
Beach Boys, the, 21, 59, 110
Beatles, the, 59, 64, 71, 83, 87, 96, 102
Before Elvis: The Prehistory of Rock 'n' Roll, 20
Belafonte, Harry, 54
"Be My Baby," 44, 45, 62
Bennett, Tony, 54
BERL Productions, 128
Berry, Chuck, 8, 48
Betrock, Alan, 43
Biello, Johnny, 73
Birnbaum, Larry, 17, 18, 20
Black Diamond Restaurant, 17
Blackwell, Bumps, 5
"Blueberry Hill," 8
Blue Cat Records, 49, 68
"Blue Monday," 8
Blue Monday: Fats Domino and the Lost Dawn of Rock 'n' Roll, 24
Bob B. Soxx and the Blue Jeans, 44
"Bony Moronie," 6
Booker T. Washington High School, 27
"Born Too Late," 69
"Bottom of My Soul," 58
Boudreaux, John, 9
"Boy from New York City, The," 49
Braun, Julius, 17
Brenner, Dr. Joseph, 33–35
Brill Building, 43, 47, 48, 53, 66, 80
Brooks, LaLa, 46
Broven, John, 19
Brimmer, Charles, 101
"Brother John," 141
Brown, Beverly, 98–102, 142
Brown, Maxine, 69
Brown, Roy, 17, 19
Brown, Ruth, 45
Bryant Hotel, 54, 55, 57
Buckwheat Zydeco, 141
Buffett, Jimmy, 141

Burdon, Eric, 87–90
Butler, Artie, 57, 68
Butler, Jerry, 9, 57
Butterflies, the, 50

"California Sun," 21
Calliope Projects, 29, 30
Cannon, Freddy, 110
"Can't Buy Me Love," 59
Capitol Records, 19
Caravan of Stars Tour, 77, 78, 96
Carter G. Woodson Junior High School, 4
Castaways, the, 93
Castro, Fidel, 115
Celestin, Oscar Philip (Papa), 24, 25, 28
Chandler, Chas, 87
Chantels, the, 45, 47
"Chapel of Love," 31, 44–47, 49, 51–54, 56, 58, 59, 61–67, 80, 94, 98, 102, 107, 110, 112, 115, 117, 127, 139, 142, 143
Charles, Ray, 59, 68, 70
"Charlie Brown," 45
Chiffons, the, 13, 45, 50
Cimino, Sam, 24
Clark, Dick, 77–80, 83, 96
Clifford, Mike, 78
Clinton, Bill, 31, 142
Coasters, the, 45, 85
Coleman, Rick, 24
Columbia Records, 24, 133
Como, Julian, 28
Connick, Harry, Jr., 131
Cooke, Sam, 5, 9
Cookies, the, 50
Coppersmith, Ted, 30
Costello, Elvis, 141
Court of the Two Sisters, 24
Cousin Brucie, 55
Crawford, James "Sugar Boy," 111, 112
Crystals, the, 44, 46, 49, 51, 52, 59, 63, 65, 78, 79, 81

"Da Doo Ron Ron," 44, 45, 51, 52, 78
Daisy Records, 45, 49
Danny & The Juniors, 68
"Danny Boy," 71
Dave Clark Five, 83

Index

David, Hal, 43
Davis, Skeeter, 13
Dean and Jean (Welton Young and Brenda Lee Jones), 78–80
Decon, Reynold, 11
"Dedicated to the One I Love," 45
DeLuxe Records, 17
DeSanto, Sugar Pie, 83
Diamond, Lee (Wilbert Smith), 69
"Diana," 68
Dillard University, 18
Dirty Dozen Brass Band, 141
Domino, Antoine "Fats," 7, 8, 18, 20, 70, 131, 142
"Don't Break My Heart," 101
Dorsey, Lee, 7, 41
Douglas, Lizzie (Memphis Minnie), 133
"Down Home Girl," 57, 58
"Down the Aisle of Love," 50
Drifters, the, 45

Eaglin, Snooks, 9
888 Building, 55
Elegants, the, 68
Emerson, Ken, 47, 51, 52
"End of the World," 13
End Records, 47

Faithful, Marianne, 83
Father of the Bride, 59
"Fat Man, The," 7
Favorite, Barbara, 11
Fedison, Harold, 69
Fields, Frank, 8, 18
Five Deejays, 12, 37, 40, 41
Flamingos, the, 9
Florida State University, 135
Floyd, King, 6, 7
Fogerty, John, 141
Fowler, Nell, 102
Freddie and the Dreamers, 110
Freeman, Bobby, 81
Full Metal Jacket, 59
Fulson, Lowell, 19

Gail, Linda, 97
Gaines, Ernestine, 41, 62

"Game of Love, The," 110
Gayten, Paul, 17, 18
"Gee the Moon Is Shining Bright," 62
Gerry & the Pacemakers, 64, 96, 97
"Girls Can Tell," 63, 65, 66
Glee, 59
Glover, Danny, 32
Glover, Henry, 21
GLOW, 59
Godchaux's (Gaucho's), 9
Goffin, Gerry, 43
Goldner, George, 20, 21, 47, 52, 67, 68
Gone Records, 47
"Go Now," 49
"Good Rockin' Tonight," 17, 19
Gordy, Barry, 70, 102
Grant, Cecil, 17
Grateful Dead, 113
Graystone, 24
Greenwich, Ellie, 43, 44, 45, 47–52, 54, 62–68, 107, 108, 110
Grier, Roosevelt, 97
"Groove Me," 7
Guardian of the Flames, 70
Guitar Slim, 41
Gunter, Cornell, 85

Hall, Clarence, 24
Hall, Reggie, 20
"Hanky Panky," 44
Hannusch, Jeff, 17, 111
"Hard Day's Night, A," 64
Harris, Wynonie, 17
Harrison, Big Chief Donald, 70
"Hatti Malatti," 69
Hawketts, the, 9
Hawkins, Barbara, 3–6, 9–12, 15, 18, 21, 23, 25, 26, 28, 29, 32, 37, 38, 39, 41, 44–46, 48, 50, 51, 53, 55, 56, 65, 68, 69, 71–75, 78, 79, 82, 84, 88–91, 95–96, 98–100, 102–5, 109, 111, 113, 115–20, 122, 125–29, 133–36, 139, 142, 144
Hawkins, Hartzell, 27
Hawkins, Lucille Cordelia Merette, 10, 12, 13, 23, 25, 26, 28, 30–35, 38, 39, 40, 53, 54, 65, 119, 134
Hawkins, Ronnie, 20

Hawkins, Shirley, 27, 134, 138
Heart of Rock & Soul: The 1001 Greatest Singles Ever Made, The, 59
"Heat Wave," 45
"Hello Dolly," 59
"Hello Mary Lou," 80
"Help Me Rhonda," 110
Hendrix, Jimi, 41
Henry, Clarence "Frogman," 141
"Here It Comes Again," 71
Herman's Hermits, 100
"He's a Rebel," 78, 80
"He's So Fine," 13, 45
"Hey Little Cobra," 78
"Hey Little Girl," 80
"Hey Paula," 13
"Hey Pocky A-Way," 70, 142
Hogan, Carl, 69, 71
Holloway, Brenda, 78, 81
Hondells, the, 110
Hopkins, Lightnin', 20
"Hound Dog," 45
"House of the Rising Sun, The," 87
Houston, William, 6
Houston's for Music, 6
"How Do You Do It," 64
Hyland, Brian, 78, 84

"I Don't Wanna Fuss," 83
"I Get Around," 59
"I Got You Babe," 62
"I Hear You Knockin'," 8
I Hear You Knockin': The Sound of New Orleans Rhythm and Blues, 18, 111
"I Just Don't Know What to Do with Myself," 83
Ike & Tina Turner, 8
"Iko Iko," 7, 63, 69, 80, 93, 94, 101, 107–13, 125, 141, 142
ILA Labor Union Hall, 6
"I Like It Like That," 57
"I'll Never Let the Well Run Dry," 71
"I'm Gone," 20
"I'm Gonna Get You Yet," 62, 110
"I'm Not the Kind of Girl (To Marry)," 71
"I'm Telling You Now," 110

"I Only Want to Be with You," 83
"(I've Got a) Uh Uh Wife," 21
"I've Got to Get That Boy," 71
"Is That All There Is?," 45
"It Ain't My Fault," 126
"It Hurts to Be in Love," 78
"I Wanna Love Him So Bad," 50
"I Want to Hold Your Hand," 59
"I Want to Know," 83

J&M Recording Studio, 17, 18
Jackson Five, 69
"Jailhouse Rock," 45
Jagger, Mick, 84, 85
"Jambalaya," 8
Jellybeans, the, 50
Jesuit High School, 135
Jim Doval & the Gauchos, 97
"Jock-A-Mo," 111
Joey Dee and the Starliters, 20, 73
John, Elton, 141
John Casablancas Centers, 31, 123
Johnson, Howard, 10
Johnson, Joan Marie, 4, 10, 15, 18, 21, 23, 37, 44, 48, 50, 51, 55, 56, 58, 68, 69, 71, 72, 74, 75, 79, 85, 86, 89–91, 95–96, 98, 101, 102, 111, 113, 115–18, 125, 126, 131, 133, 139, 142, 143
Johnson, Lyndon B., 93
Johnson, Joseph "Smokey," 66, 126
Johnson, Sporty, 17
Johnson, Mr. and Mrs. William, 65
Jones, Alice, 16
Jones, Annabell, 16
Jones, Bernadine, 16
Jones, Brian, 84
Jones, Charles, 16
Jones, Deborah, 71
Jones, Joe, 11–13, 15–19, 23, 37, 40, 41, 42, 43, 48, 51, 55–58, 65–69, 71–75, 78, 82, 83, 85–91, 94, 101–4, 111, 113, 118, 119, 125–31
Jones, Joe, Jr., 71
Jones, Marilyn, 69, 71, 85, 88
Jones, Myrtle, 17
Jones, Sharon, 71
Jones, Tom, 96
Juilliard Conservatory of Music, 16

"Junker Blues," 7
"Just Like Romeo and Juliet," 78

Kaiser University, 135
Kasuals, the, 78, 81
K-Doe, Ernie, 7, 142, 143
Kennedy, Carolyn, 34
Kennedy, John F., 116
Kennedy, John. F., Jr., 34
Kenner, Chris, 57
Kenniebrew, Dolores "Dee Dee," 79
"Kind of Boy You Can't Forget, The," 63
King, B.B., 19, 70
King, Ben E., 45
King, Carole, 43
King, Earl, 41, 61, 62, 66
King, Martin Luther, 93
Kingston Trio, 45
Kinks, the, 83
Knight, Jean, 7
Knox, Buddy, 20
Ku Klux Klan, 93, 98, 101

Lance, Major, 78, 80, 81, 110
Landers, Ann, 53
"Land of 1,000 Dances," 57
Lastie, Melvin, 18, 74
Lastie, David, 18
Lastie, Joe, 18
Lauper, Cyndi, 141, 142
Laurie, Annie, 18
"Leader of the Pack," 50
Led Zeppelin, 133
Lee, Peggy, 45
Legend, 59
Leiber, Jerry, 45–59, 64, 67–69, 107, 108, 110, 111
Leon, Bonnie, 112
"Let the Good Times Roll," 19
Levy, Morris, 20
Lioness Club, 31, 32
"Little Bell," 63, 67, 110
Little David and the Wanderers, 93
Little Miss and the Muffets, 50
Little Richard, 8, 18
"Little Star," 68
Lorets, the, 11

Louisiana State University, 135
Louisiana Treasures Hall of Fame, 144
Louisiana World Exposition, 129
Love, Darlene, 44, 46
"Love Is Strange," 40
"Love Me Do," 59
"Love Me with All Your Heart," 59
"Love on a Two-Way Street," 40
"Lovey Dovey Pair," 11
"Lucky Lips," 45

Macy's, 46
Madison Square Garden, 141
Malaco Records, 7
Manfred Mann, 78
"(Man Who Shot) Liberty Valance," 80
Margaret, Princess, 83
"Marie Laveau," 25
Marion (girlfriend), 88, 104
Marion Military Institute, 135
Marsalis, Branford, 131
Marsden, Gerry, 97
Marsh, Dave, 59
Martha & the Vandellas, 45, 72
Massachusetts Institute of Technology, 134
Matassa, Cosimo, 18, 20
Mathis, Johnny, 48
Maurice Williams & the Zodiacs, 20
"Maybe," 45, 47
McCannon, George, 78, 81
McCartney, Paul, 83, 85
McCoy, "Kansas" Joe, 133
McGuire Sisters, 69
McKinley, Larry, 7, 11
Melder, Edmund (Joe Jones), 71
Melder Publishing Co., 71, 113, 125, 126
Meltones, the, 4, 6, 9, 11, 37, 40, 41, 44, 45, 50
Merette, Cordelia (grandmother), 25–28
Merette, Ernest, 29
Merette, Joe, 26, 27
Merette, Willie, 29
Mesner, Eddie, 20
Meters, the, 70, 141, 142
Mickey & Sylvia, 12, 40
Midler, Bette, 141
Mills, Eleanore, 102–4
Minit Records, 7, 8

Mirasound Studios, 51, 107
Miss Henry (music teacher), 3
Mission Impossible 2, 113
Moments, the, 40
"Monkey Time, The," 80
Morris, Leo (Idris Muhammad), 9
Morton, George "Shadow," 50
"Mother-in-Law," 7, 143
Motown Records, 71, 102, 110
"Mr. Big Stuff," 7
"Mrs. Brown You've Got a Lovely Daughter," 110
Murray the K, 55
MusiCares, 143
"My Boyfriend's Back," 45
"My Boy Lollipop," 59
"My Dad," 80
"My Guy," 59

National Academy of Recording Arts, 143
Negro Musicians Union, 19
Nelson, Benjamin, 27, 28
Nelson, Bessie, 27
Nelson, Elnorie, 27
Nelson, Julia, 27
Nelson, Willie, 97
Neville, Aaron, 5, 6, 7, 8, 57, 136, 138, 139, 142
Neville, Arthur, 5, 6, 8, 9, 51, 56, 70
Neville, Athelgra, 5, 39, 142, 144
Neville, Charles, 56, 57
Neville, Joel, 136, 138, 142
Neville, Little Aaron, 137
Neville, Mommee, 5
Neville Brothers, 5, 6, 128, 131, 141, 142
Newbeats, the, 96
Newman, Paul, 142
New Orleans Jazz & Heritage Festival, 128, 131, 144
New Orleans Saints, 31
New Orleans Walk of Fame, 144
Norton, Major General John, 95
"Nowhere to Run," 72

Oberman, Ronnie, 112
Ogden, Bob, 17
Okeh Records, 24
"One Big Mouth," 21

O'Neil, Jimmy, 80, 96, 97, 133
"Only Love Can Break a Heart," 80
"Over You," 5, 7

Paddock Lounge, 24
Paige, Joey, 97
Palmer, Earl, 8, 18
Parker, Robert, 66
Parnell, Alma, 17
Pastor's Aid Choir, 26
Paul and Paula, 13
"People," 59
"People Get Ready," 70
"People Say," 52, 63–65, 67, 80, 83, 110
Peppermint Lounge, 73
Peter and Gordon, 59, 96
Peters, Ron, 96, 98, 99, 101, 119, 127
Peterson, Paul, 80, 81
Phillips, Barbara, 4, 5
"Pillow Talk," 40
Pitney, Gene, 78, 80, 83
Poni-Tails, 69
Powers, Tony, 44
Presley, Elvis, 45
Preston, Billy, 66
Price, Alan, 87
Professor Longhair, 144

Quezergue, Wardell, 7, 51, 66, 71, 101, 126
Quin-Tones, the, 50

Raindrops, the, 63
"Rapper's Delight," 40
Ready Steady Go!, 83
Rebirth Brass Band, 141
Rebennack, Mac (Dr. John), 6, 7, 19, 131, 142
Red Bird Records, 45, 49, 52, 54–58, 61–64, 67–69, 72, 107, 109, 110, 112, 127
Reese, Della, 54
Reflections, the, 78
"Remember (Walking in the Sand)," 50
"Reverend Mr. Black," 45
Rhythm & Blues Hall of Fame, 144
Ric Records, 20, 21
Riding High, 69–71
Rip Chords, the, 78
Ripp, Artie, 50

Rivieras, the, 21
Robichaux, Joe, 24
Robin Hood Club, 17
Robinson, Alvin, 57, 58
Robinson, Joseph, 40
Rodgers, Jimmie, 20
Rolling Stones, 58, 64, 83, 84, 110
Ronettes, the, 44, 46, 49, 52, 59, 63, 73
Ross, Diana, 79, 102. *See also* Supremes, the
Roulette Records, 20, 47
Round Robin, 78
Rubens at the Palace, the, 85
Ruffins, Kermit, 141
Rupe, Art, 6

Saint Augustine High School, 10, 11, 37
Saint John's Lutheran, 134, 135
Saint Mark's Baptist Church, 26, 30, 31
Sands, Evie, 49
Savoy Records, 11
"Shake a Hand," 20
"Sha-La-La," 78
Shangri-Las, the, 50, 68
Shaw, Sandy, 83
"She Loves You," 59
Shindig!, 66, 83, 96, 133
Shirelles, the, 45, 50, 61, 78, 81
Shirley & Lee (Shirley Goodman and Leonard Lee), 19, 20
Shivaree, 110
Sho-Bar, 6
"Short Fat Fannie," 6
Sia, 113
Simon & Garfunkel, 141
Sinatra, Frank, 57
"Since I Fell for You," 18
1650 Broadway, 43
Small, Millie, 59
"Soldier Boy," 45
"Something You Got," 57
Sonny & Cher, 62
Southern University, 26, 38, 39, 116, 128
Spartan's Department Store, 72
Specialty Records, 6, 8
Spector, Phil, 44, 46, 49, 51, 52, 59, 62, 63, 67
Spector, Ronnie (Veronica), 52, 62
Springfield, Dusty, 83

"Stand by Me," 45
"Stay," 20
Steele, John, 87
Stephen X (boyfriend), 116, 117
Stoller, Mike, 45–53, 55–59, 64, 66–69, 108, 110, 111
"Stop! In the Name of Love," 72
Streisand, Barbra, 59
"Sugah Wooga," 4
Sugar Hill Gang, 40
Sugar Hill Records, 40
"Sunny Side of the Street, The," 31
Superdome, 31
Supremes, the, 71, 72, 78, 79, 81, 110
"Surfin'," 21
Sylvania F. Williams Elementary School, 30
Syria Mosque, 81

"Take Me for a Little While," 49
"Teasin' You," 6
Tee, Willie, 6
"Tell It Like It Is," 57
"Tell Me," 64
"Thank You Mama, Thank You Papa," 41–43, 62
"That's Where It's At," 69
"Then He Kissed Me," 44, 52, 78
"There Goes My Baby," 45
Thomas, Irma, 131, 141, 142
Thompson, Sue, 97
"Three O'Clock Blues," 19
Three Playmates, 4, 11
"Ticket to Ride," 110
Tico Records, 47
Tiger Records, 45, 49, 57
Tiny Tim, 49
Tipitina's, 144
"(Today I Met) The Boy I'm Gonna Marry," 44
Tommy James & the Shondells, 44
"Tonight's the Night," 61
Toussaint, Allen, 8, 9, 128, 141
"Town without Pity," 80
Toys, the, 50
"True," 18
Tulane University, 135
Tulane University School of Medicine, 33

Tuxedo Dance Hall, 24
Tuxedo Jazz Band (Tuxedo Brass Band), 24
"Two-Way-Poc-Away," 66, 69, 70, 110
Tyler, Alvin "Red," 5, 18

"Um Um Um Um Um Um," 80

Valdee, LaRay, 78
Valentine, Hilton, 87
Vanderbilt University, 135
Vanderpool (Robinson), Sylvia, 12, 23, 40, 41, 46
Vee-Jay Records, 69
Ventures, the, 64
Vial, Mr. and Mrs. Ulric, 30
Vietnam (War), 93–96, 102
Vocal Group Hall of Fame, 144
Voting Rights Act, 93, 96

"Walk Don't Run '64," 64
"Walking to New Orleans," 8
"Walking with Mr. Lee," 18
Walter Louis Cohn High School (Wa-Lo-Co), 3, 4, 5
Ward, Ed, 18
Warwick, Dionne, 43
Washington, Baby, 69
Washington, Wallace, 27
Wayne Fontana and the Mindbenders, 110
Welch, Lenny, 18
Welcome to Marwen, 59
Wells, Mary, 59
Westerly, 55
Westmoreland, General William, 94–96
"What a Guy," 63
"What Comes Up, Must Come Down," 69, 71
"What's Going On," 6
"When Your Hair Has Turned to Silver," 20
"When the Levee Breaks," 133
"Where Did Our Love Go," 78
"Why Don't They Let Us Fall in Love," 62, 63
William Morris Agency Inc., 77, 83
"Will You Love Me Tomorrow," 43, 45
Wilson, Mary, 79
"Wishin' and Hopin'," 83
Wholesale Fur Company, 16
"Why Do Lovers Break Each Other's Hearts," 44
Williams, Larry, 6
Woolworth's, 39
World Cotton Centennial of 1884, 130
"World without Love, A," 59

"Ya Ya," 7
"You Done Me Wrong," 20
"You Don't Love Me," 18
Young, Inell, 128
"You Send Me," 5
"You Should Have Seen the Way He Looked at Me," 63, 68, 93, 110
"You Talk Too Much," 15, 18, 20, 21, 23, 41, 65

Zeldman, Maurice and Seymour, 54

ABOUT THE AUTHORS

Rosa Hawkins (Tampa, Florida) was one of the three original members of the Dixie Cups. She still performs with the group today.

Steve Bergsman (Mesa, Arizona) is a longtime journalist who has written over a dozen books. His most recent book was a biography of Screamin' Jay Hawkins.